Wonderfully made

Wonderfully made

Dr A. J. Monty White

EVANGELICAL PRESS

EVANGELICAL PRESS
12 Wooler Street, Darlington, Co. Durham, DL1 1RQ, England

© Evangelical Press 1989
First published 1989

British Library Cataloguing in Publication Data available

ISBN 0 85234 262 4

Printed in Great Britain by The Bath Press, Avon.

For Simon,

Rebekah

and Paul

Know ye that the Lord he is God:

it is he that hath made us,

and not we ourselves.

King David in Psalm 100 verse 3
(Authorized Version)

Contents

1.
Does it matter?

Does it matter what we believe about our origins? Does what we believe affect our everyday lives? If so, how? Is the creation/evolution debate an important issue? What is it all about? Does it affect us? These are some of the questions that I want us to address in the introduction to this book on human origins, and it is my hope that we will find some meaningful answers to these and other similar questions.

First of all, let me state that we should not think that all evolutionists are atheists. Some evolutionists do have an intellectual belief in the existence of God even though they do not know him as their Lord and Saviour. Other evolutionists do know God as their Lord and Saviour, and although they may not accept a literal interpretation of the Genesis account of the creation and early history of the earth, they do regard God as the Creator; but they believe that he created using evolutionary processes.

Some atheistic evolutionists, however, have put forward evolutionary explanations to account for people's belief in God. The late Sir Julian Huxley, for instance, maintained that God is the creation of man![1] He argued that as ape-like animals evolved into people, their brains evolved a consciousness which in turn evolved a religion together with an associated deity or deities. Hence for Sir Julian Huxley, God is the product of evolution! Jacques Monod, on the other hand, considers that the idea of God is the product of a chance myth-prescribing mutation in the human genetic code.[2] In other words, for such atheist evolutionists, God does not exist - he is no more than the product of the human imagination.

It is because of ideas such as those of Huxley and Monod that some of the dangers inherent in the theory of evolution become apparent. The theory of evolution can be used to dethrone the Lord God Almighty from his glorious position as the Creator of all things. Indeed, Sir Julian Huxley is on record as saying that he was an atheist and that Darwin's real achievement was to remove the whole idea of God as the Creator of organisms from the sphere of rational discussion.[3] In other words, Sir Julian Huxley thought that when the subject of origins was considered, the Originator should not be considered, for it was his belief that the Creator was no more than a figment of the imagination.

Darwin and his theory of evolution have now taken the place of God. Everything (including God) can be explained in terms of evolution - even the evidence that does not fit the theory.[4] To show that Darwin and his theory are held in such high regard by so many evolutionists, allow me to quote Dr Colin Patterson of the British Museum (Natural History): 'Just as pre-Darwinian biology was carried out by people whose faith was in the Creator and His plan, post-Darwinian biology is being carried out by people whose faith is in, almost, the deity of Darwin.'[5] This should make us wonder whether those people who hold Darwin and his theory in such high regard are really objective in their scientific teaching and research.

Now it is the anti-God element of evolutionary teaching that should concern us. Let me stress again, I know that not all evolutionists are atheists, but taken to its logical conclusion, evolution does not require a Creator because according to evolution *everything* is the result of chance natural processes. If evolution were true, what need would there be for a God? Surely the pronouncements of the atheistic evolutionists about God's existing only in people's imagination would then gain credibility. The One who claims to have created all things would simply not exist! No wonder the late Sir Cecil Wakeley, past President of the Royal College of Surgeons said, 'The theory of evolution is the gospel of the atheist and paves the way to the complete rejection of the Bible.'[6]

Humanism is the religion of the atheist and it uses evolution as its Bible, as we can see by looking at the first and second affirmations of the Humanist Manifesto:

   '*Affirmation 1:* Religious humanists regard the universe as
      self-existing and not created.
   '*Affirmation 2:* Humanism believes that man is a part of nature

and that he has emerged as the result of a continuous process.'

Humanists, therefore, are people who do not believe in God, but instead believe in people. This means that humanists do not look for guidance to any supernatural source, but to human warmth, intelligence, creativity and concern. They believe that life and its relationships are supposed to involve a struggle and a search through which both growth and happiness can be experienced. Even though the number of humanists in the UK is and always has been small, over the last hundred years humanists have had a profound effect upon the society in which we live.

Now even though humanists accept the concept of 'the open society', in which every viewpoint is allowed free expression and development, limited only by the rights of others, humanists tend to be very anti-Christian and anti-God. The opposition by humanists to the 'Jesus is Alive!' postmark to celebrate Easter in 1988 is a case in point. Pick up any humanist publication and the anti-Christian nature of humanism is very evident. Articles attacking such things as the historicity of the Lord Jesus Christ and the authenticity of the Scriptures seem to take up a disproportionate amount of space. Why is there such an attack on God, his Word and his Son? I am sure that one of the most convincing arguments for the existence of God is the anti-God attitude of so many people. Why is it that atheists are not content with just not believing in God? Why is it that they are so anti-God? Why do they oppose someone that they do not believe exists? If God did not exist, then such an attitude would be insane.

In spite of their idea that every viewpoint should be allowed free expression and development, humanists do not extend this courtesy to Christianity in particular, nor to religion in general. According to Barbara Smoker humanists 'are opposed to the dogmatic teaching of religion in state schools'.[7] This opposition is very real. In a circular letter sent out in 1981, Kenneth Furnes, the General Secretary of the British Humanist Association, stated: 'One major campaign in which we are engaged at present and which you have probably read all about in the press is our attempt to alter the 1944 Education Act to bring about a rational, open and educational approach to the teaching of belief systems in schools in place of religious indoctrination. This has brought us a great deal of support and if successful would bring about a radical change in society in a very few years.'

It is not only compulsory Religious Education and morning worship in schools that humanists oppose. In a circular letter dated 7 November 1980 from Betty James, Membership Secretary of the British Humanist Association, it was stated that they also wish to challenge 'the still enormous power and privileges of the church'. State-supported church schools and religious broadcasting were stated as specific examples.

Humanists' views opposing religious instruction in schools are shared by others. For example, I have been informed by an organization called 'Campaign Against Christian Indoctrination in County Schools' that it will take legal proceedings against me if I continue to teach creationism at Christian Union meetings, Religious Education lessons and General Study lessons in county secondary schools.

Needless to say, humanists are evolutionists believing that the future evolution of this planet rests in our own hands. To guide us in this task, and also in our own personal life, humanists teach that we need values. And where do these values come from? Well, according to the British Humanist Association's introduction to humanism called *The Humanist Perspective*, these values were 'discovered during evolution' and 'such values include telling the truth, being honest, accepting responsibility, playing fair, co-operation for the common good and caring for others'. One wonders whether the author of this paper has ever heard of evolutionary concepts such as 'the survival of the fittest' or 'the selfish gene'!

This aspect of humanistic philosophy is, of course, contrary to the Christian teaching about the creation and fall of man. And it is the whole concept of sin that is at the heart of the whole creation/ evolution debate. Nigel Cameron has summed up the key question as follows: 'Do men die because of sin, or do they die because they are men? That is, is mortality *natural,* or is it *moral?* According to evolution it has to be natural, since - however the first man came to be - he was mortal already. He was the child of animal parents who were, of course, mortal themselves.'[8]

According to the Bible, the first humans were created perfect, but through disobedience fell from this original perfect sinless state. Because of the first person's disobedience everyone is disobedient to God. No one can ever attain the perfection in this life that the first human couple once had, no matter how hard he or she tries. We are all sinners. Yet God has not abandoned us, but sent his only begotten Son, that whosoever believes in him, should not perish, but have everlasting life.[9]

In the British Humanist Association's introduction to humanism called *The Humanist Perspective*, it is stated that 'Religions have sustained some important human values but, because they are founded on supernatural conceptions and, often, on the idea of an absolutely perfect divine being, they tend by nature to be authoritarian and divisive and have often opposed the emergence of new truth. We cannot, then, look to established religions to give the modern world the moral foundation that it needs. Respect for human values and for life offers the best hope of working towards a world-wide morality.'

Today our country is reaping the fruits of humanistic and evolutionary teachings like this that have been sown for years by our educational establishments and by the media. Abortion on demand, easy divorce, homosexuality, lesbianism, pornography and lawlessness are the fruits of a society that does not know the Lord. The majority of people reject God's Word and the Author of that Word. Many people simply do not believe in God, and it is only a minority who worship him in spirit and in truth.

Now the theory of evolution teaches that human beings are the product of chance natural processes without the intervention of any supernatural agent. This is in complete contrast to the Bible, where we read that God supernaturally created the first human pair. Now because evolution is believed by so many scientists, the average person supposes that there are scientific reasons for believing in evolution and therefore that there must be scientific reasons for rejecting the Bible and, consequently, God.

Many people now reason in this way. Furthermore, some argue that if we are just animals, the result of random natural processes, then why should abortion, or even euthanasia, be considered wrong? Putting to death an unwanted puppy or kitten is not considered immoral, so why is it wrong for an unwanted unborn child? Putting to death an old sick dog or cat is considered a kind act, so why not perform a similar 'kind act' to an old sick person? Indeed, we can appreciate their arguments, for if we are just animals, and there is no God, then there is no God to sin against. Hence we can see how a 'do-as-you-please-so-long-as-no-one-gets-hurt' society can come about. And this is the type of society that we are experiencing today: millions of unborn children are being murdered; thousands of couples are living together in an unmarried state; hundreds of acts of immorality are being performed. This is, I believe, as a direct result of people accepting a theory of origins that eliminates all references to God.

At the same time, and as a consequence of rejecting the Word of God, the family is under attack. I have already mentioned the fact that many couples are living together in an unmarried state. Feminists argue that mothers do not *naturally* have a maternal role to play in rearing their children, maintaining that this role is thrust upon them by men in a male-dominated society! Such an argument is nonsensical and is clearly contrary to nature. However, some feminists argue that the role of the father is redundant and they are perfectly happy to be artificially inseminated in order to conceive a child and to bring up a child without the aid of a male companion. Furthermore, feminists attack the idea of the father-figure of God, demanding that he should be referred to in the feminine form. Feminists' views are clearly contrary to the Word of God. However, in passing, I do wish that men would read and study what the Word of God tells them about their role in the family - and then put it into practice!

There has also been a tremendous increase in pornography in recent years. What was considered obscene thirty years ago is now 'acceptable'. Some try to argue that there is no harm in pornography. However, in their book *Take Back the Night,* the authors show the damaging effects that pornography has on society.[10] Pornography is not love, it is sin; it not only includes lust, but also hatred. It degrades women, in that they are no longer seen as man's partners, but as objects or, more often, slaves to man's every sexual desire.

Some would accuse me of blaming all of society's ills on the theory of evolution. This would be an oversimplification. The case that I am trying to make, however, is that people use this theory to give them an excuse to reject God and his laws. It is of our own free will that we reject God and his laws - the rules that he has given us so that we can lead lives that are pleasing to him. When we buy a new piece of equipment for our home, we are given the maker's instructions which tell us what to do and what not to do with it. So it is with us, for God has given us the Maker's instructions for our own lives; it is called the Bible.[11] My advice is 'Read it!'

Why then another book on the subject of origins? Well, as we have already seen, it is an important subject which has implications for all aspects of our lives. Furthermore, this book specifically deals with the subject of our own origins and its purpose is to show that there is no real evidence for the evolution of human beings; much of what is purported to be evidence is mere conjecture, and only exists in the imagination of the evolutionist. As a result of reading this book, it is my sincere hope that you, dear reader, will come to the same conclusion that I have done, and that you will be able to say with the psalmist of old that we are 'fearfully and wonderfully made'.[12]

2.
What are the differences?

Before we look at the evidence that is available about our origins, it is important for us to remind ourselves what we mean by creation and what we mean by evolution, so that we can see for ourselves the fundamental differences in the two accounts of origins.

The account of the creation of the universe, the sun, moon and stars by Almighty God is found in Genesis chapter 1. The account of how he created plants and animals to reproduce after their own kind is also found in this first chapter of the Bible. A detailed account of the creation of the first human couple is found in Genesis chapter 2, where we read in verse 7 that God formed the first man, Adam 'from the dust of the ground and breathed into his nostrils the breath of life, and the man became a living being'. However, Adam did not have a partner, 'so the Lord God caused the man to fall into a deep sleep; and while he was sleeping, he took one of the man's ribs [or part of the man's side (footnote)] and closed up the place with flesh. Then the Lord God made a woman from the rib [or part (footnote)] he had taken out of the man, and he brought her to the man' (Genesis 2:21-22). Adam's partner was called Eve. Adam and Eve were the first human couple.

Having briefly described the creation of our ancestors, I hope that the reader will forgive me if I give a fairly full account of what evolutionists teach about the origins of things in general, and about the origin of people in particular. In order to help with the concept of the evolutionary time-scale and the order of events which are supposed to have occurred within it, a calendar of evolution has been included. If you are familiar with the evolutionary account of

CALENDAR OF EVOLUTION

Number of years ago	Geological Period (if relevant)	Significant Evolutionary Event
12,000,000,000		Big bang giving rise to the universe
4,600,000,000		Condensation of sun and planets, including the earth
3,600,000,000		First self-replicating organism
3,500,000,000		Evolution of bacteria
2,500,000,000		Cyanobacteria (blue-green algae) evolved
1,500,000,000		Eukaryotic cells formed
1,000,000,000		Evolution of simple invertebrates, such as sponges
700,000,000	Late Precambrian	Evolution of complex invertebrates such as jellyfish
480,000,000	Ordovician	Fish evolved
400,000,000	Early Devonian	Lobed-finned fish developed
360,000,000	Late Devonian	Amphibians developed
260,000,000	Early Permian	Reptiles emerged
200,000,000	Triassic	Mammals arose
70,000,000	Early Eocene	The prosimians, the first primates evolved
50,000,000	Late Eocene	Monkeys evolved
35,000,000	Oligocene	Old World Monkeys/New World Monkeys split
25,000,000	Early Miocene	Early apes evolved
15,000,000	Miocene	Ramapithecines lived
4,000,000		Australopithecines evolved
2,000,000		The habilines arose
1,500,000		*Homo erectus* people developed
150,000		Early *Homo sapiens* people evolved
40,000		*Homo sapiens sapiens* (i.e. modern people) arose
10,000		The agricultural revolution occurred

our origins, or if you find such an account difficult to follow because of the scientific terms and concepts, then my advice would be to turn to the last paragraph of this chapter, not forgetting to look at the cartoon and captions on page 27.

Evolutionists believe that our species is the result of chance natural processes which began with a big bang that occurred about twelve thousand million years ago.[1] Evolutionary cosmologists believe that all the matter in the universe was once in the same place at the same time, and that at time zero (i.e. the beginning) this primeval atom, as it is called, exploded and began to expand. The universe as it is today is therefore believed to be the result of the explosion and subsequent expansion of that primeval atom. Where the initial matter-energy primeval atom came from is a matter of conjecture, as is what made it become unstable and caused it to explode and subsequently expand. Now the astronomers believe that what we call 'empty space' is part and parcel of the universe, and so it was also part and parcel of the primeval atom. Hence it is believed that the primeval atom did not expand into what we call empty space, but into what may be called 'a void', i.e. a concept of absolute nothingness - not even empty space!

It is believed that as the universe has expanded, stars have formed, and that thousands of millions of these stars have grouped themselves together into galaxies. It is also believed that star formation and extinction (or death) continue to occur in the thousands of millions of galaxies which are known to exist in the universe. The expansion of the universe and its subsequent evolution is believed to be continuing today. According to some, this expansion will continue until all the stars die and a state of infinite rarefaction is reached in ten to the power ten to the power of seventy-six years' time.[2] Others believe that the universe will eventually collapse and form another primeval atom which will then explode and produce another universe, which in turn will collapse and explode to form yet another universe, and so on *ad infinitum.*

The formation, evolution and death of stars is crucial in the evolutionary account of the origin of people, for according to this account, it is the stars themselves that provide all the elements that we find on the earth today and which are crucial for life itself. It is believed that elements are formed in a step-wise process known as 'nuclear fusion' in the intensely hot interiors of stars. This basic process, which also keeps stars hot inside, is the fusion of hydrogen nuclei (protons) to make helium. The net result is that four protons are converted into one helium-4 nucleus (2 protons + 2 neutrons), liberating two positrons (e^+), a couple of neutrinos, and energy in the form of gamma rays. The positrons soon meet up with electrons and annihilate, releasing still more energy.

Once helium-4 is present, it becomes the basic stepping stone to produce heavier elements. For example, three atoms of helium-4 will combine to give one atom of carbon-12; an atom of silicon-28 plus seven atoms of helium-4 will combine to give one atom of nickel-56; nickel-56 will then give cobalt-56 which in turn will give iron-56. These latter reactions occur at a temperature of about two thousand million degrees. Iron-56 is the most stable element and the heaviest that can be built by fusion reactions that release energy. To synthesize heavier elements, energy has to be put *into* the reactions. This happens when stars explode. It should be noted that although over seventy elements have been spectroscopically identified in the sun, and although it is fairly certain that nuclear fusion occurs not only in the sun but also in other stars, there is no proof that *all* of the elements everywhere came from such a process.

The history of a star is thought to be successive stages of internal gravitational contraction and thermonuclear burning. When stars explode (as *novae* or *supernovae*) they scatter their elements into space. It is believed that as new stars form, they absorb these earlier formed element debris and so are able to extend the nuclear fusion process (provided, of course, that the stars are at the right temperature) to synthesize even heavier elements. It is thought that by the time the solar system formed nearly five thousand million years ago, all of the elements that we now find in it (including all those in and on earth) had been formed in the birth and death of stars.

Of all the ideas put forward by evolutionary astronomers of how the solar system might have formed, the most popular is that it condensed from a vast disc-shaped cloud of gas and dust, which gradually contracted under its own gravity to form the sun and its family of planets. It is believed that the sun formed from the central mass when it became hot enough for thermonuclear reactions to take place as it heated up due to gravitational contraction. This resulted in the melting of the rocky interiors of the surrounding condensations, which eventually became the planets.

Evolutionists believe that as the molten earth cooled, the crust which formed was repeatedly cracked and remelted causing a lighter granitic liquid to separate out, and that this gave rise to the continental crust. They also believe that vast amounts of gases, including water vapour, were exhaled from the semi-molten surface of the early earth, and that these gases gave rise to the earth's early atmosphere and, as the earth cooled, its surface water. It is believed that it rained for millions of years, and so erosional processes began.

Evolutionists think that the atmosphere of the pre-biotic (i.e. pre-life) earth was composed of methane, ammonia, hydrogen and water vapour. Because volcanic gases are poor in oxygen, it is believed that the pre-biotic earth's atmosphere was virtually oxygen-free. Hence there would have been no ozone[3] layer around the earth and so ultra-violet radiation from the sun could have penetrated this atmosphere. This ultra-violet radiation together with electrical discharges (i.e. lightning) caused the components in the atmosphere to react together to form amino acids, sugars and nucleic acid bases; such chemicals being the basic building blocks of life. The chemicals fell into the oceans where a 'soup' of these life-chemicals formed. Evolutionists believe that after concentration by evaporation, freezing or adsorption onto the surface of a mineral such as clay, these chemicals reacted together to produce more complex chemicals such as proteins and polysaccharides (such as starch and cellulose). It is believed that when the earth was just over one thousand million years old, (i.e. about three thousand six hundred million years ago) a self-replicating molecule (probably a double stranded nucleic acid) was eventually produced. The nucleic acid then developed the ability to manufacture and utilize proteins and these proteins formed a protective sheath around the nucleic acid like a modern virus.

It is also believed that the proteins in turn developed the ability to catalyse a variety of reactions, which are important to the replication of the nucleic acid. These include unzipping and reforming reactions of the nucleic acid itself, as well as the synthesis and degradation of other proteins, which were found to be useful in accelerating the whole replication process. In other words, the proteins became enzymes.

As the system became more complex and complicated, more space was required and so it is believed that the protein envelope expanded and so a bacterium-like cell was produced. These cells obtained their energy by a process of fermentation. It is believed, however, that a new energy-producing process evolved - that of photosynthesis, a process which derives energy from the sun and thus enables the cell to make food in and for itself. The anaerobic photosynthetic bacteria evolved first, then several hundred million years later, the cyanobacteria (i.e. the blue-green algae) evolved. Evolutionists believe that with the evolution of the cyanobacteria, oxygen was released into the atmosphere and that this caused two things to happen. The first is that because many of the living organisms on the earth at that time were unable to live in an oxygen-containing atmosphere, they died as the oxygen level in the atmosphere rose. The second is that an ozone layer formed in the upper atmosphere around the earth thus shielding it from ultra-violet radiation, and so stopping the synthesis of life from non-life ever occurring naturally upon the earth again.

The next important step in the evolution of life on earth is thought to have occurred about one thousand, five hundred million years ago when eukaryotic cells developed. The nucleic acid became concentrated and organized in chromosomes in a separate structure within the cell, called the nucleus, and specialized structures developed within the cytoplasm (the region between the cell wall and the nucleus) to undertake the routine reactions involved in energy production and other vital processes. According to the evolutionist, over the next five hundred million years some of these eukaryotic organisms began to reproduce sexually, so that shuffling and exchange of genes between like organisms occurred. It is believed that the diversification of eukaryotic organisms led to the emergence of very simple multi-cellular organisms, such as the sponges, about a thousand million years ago.

It is thought that soft-bodied invertebrates, such as the jellyfish, evolved about seven hundred million years ago. Unlike the so-called early sponges, jellyfish are a true muti-cellular organism with cells that cannot survive independently. Jellyfish are complex multi-cellular organisms composed of cells which are specialized so that the organism has muscles, a nervous system and is able to defend itself by stinging its enemy.

According to evolutionists, a hundred million years later, in the so-called Cambrian Period, animals with durable skeletons had evolved: shelled creatures such as the brachiopods; radially symmetrical organisms such as the crinoids; and elongated animals with segmented bodies such as the trilobites. Evolutionists believe that the seas of that time teemed with literally millions of complex life-forms.

Evolutionists also believe that at that time animals were evolving different modes of life and one of these developed a swimming way of life. It is believed that this animal evolved a dorsal cord which was stiff but flexible together with the characteristic chevron-shaped blocks of muscles that caused the cord to flex from side to side so as to enable the animal to swim. It is believed that eventually the animal evolved into a fish with an internal axial skeleton which had articulated vertebrae with elongated lateral flanges which supported the body walls. According to evolutionists, the first fish were armour-plated, jawless and their fins were unpaired, but within a hundred thousand years (i.e. by the so-called Devonian Period), it is believed that fish had evolved jaws, and that their fins had become paired.

One of the major types of jawed fishes was the so-called lobed-finned fish, which had bony supports within their fins. From one type of these lobed-finned fish, it is believed that the amphibians developed. Evolutionists believe that this occurred as a result of prolonged dry spells at the end of the so-called Devonian Period. It is believed that at such times, the freshwater lakes and pools, in which these lobed-finned fish lived, dried up and that some of the lobed-finned fish adapted to these drier conditions. Their bony fins were supposed to enable them to crawl and stagger over the dry areas between the pools or over the dry flats in search of food. As a new way of life slowly developed, the lobed-finned fish are supposed to have evolved into amphibians. Now amphibians are different from fish - they have two pairs of limbs; lungs with nostrils which open into the mouth cavity and which have valves to exclude water; a stronger skeleton which is able to support the weight of the animal on land; a moist glandular skin; a different circulatory system; a different nervous system; new muscles, and so on. Evolutionists believe that these changes occurred over a period of several million years, so that by the end of the so-called

Devonian Period (i.e. about three hundred and fifty million years ago), amphibians began the conquest of the land.

About ninety million years later, in the so-called early Permian Period, evolutionists think that the amphibians evolved into reptiles by the development of an egg, in which the embryo could grow, and out of which the young could hatch while the egg was in a terrestrial environment. Because this meant that the reptiles did not have to return to water in order to reproduce, it is believed that the real conquest of the land could now really begin.

Because reptiles do not have an internal temperature regulator, they are described as being 'cold-blooded'. Their body heat is determined by their surroundings and they control it by moving between sun and shade. They are unable to cool down by perspiring since their skins have no sweat glands - in fact their skin is dry and scaly to prevent water loss. In contrast to reptiles, who exist on very little food, mammals burn fuel at a rapid rate to maintain a constant high temperature. This is advantageous as it permits them greater activity than reptiles, since they can function well in cold and hot climates and still keep their temperature at its proper level. Mammals are usually furry animals to prevent heat loss when in cold places and they are able to cool down when they are hot by means of sweating.

Evolutionists teach that the mammals evolved from the reptiles during the so-called Triassic Period, some two hundred million years ago. They think that the first mammals were the small animals called the therapids (no bigger than rats and mice), most of which are thought to have been aggressive meat-eaters. Because only the hard parts (i.e. bones and teeth) of the therapids have been fossilized, it is not known whether they were indeed mammals because it is impossible to tell whether they were warm-blooded and had fur instead of scales or whether they nursed their young.

Evolutionists believe, however, that as the mammals evolved, they lived different lives from those of the reptiles: it is taught that some hunted the insects that dwelt in the undergrowth of the tropical jungles that existed at those times, while some took to the trees. In the unstable environment of the tree-tops, which makes such rigorous demands on the co-ordination of the eyes with the muscles which control locomotion, evolutionists believe that these early tree-dwelling mammals began to develop a complex brain that is the distinguishing feature of the primates. The first primates, the prosimians, are thought to have evolved about seventy million years ago.

Unlike other tree-dwelling mammals such as squirrels, which climb trees by digging their claws into the bark of the tree, it is believed that the prosimians climbed by grasping. It is also believed that they had a long snout, a wet muzzle and sensory whiskers. Evolutionists believe, however, that over a period of time some lost the projecting snout and acquired a flatter face, and that with this went a change in the position of the eyes, so that the animal began to look forward and hence have stereoscopic vision. It is believed that the fingers and toes also changed: they began to grow longer and develop as flesh pads protected on the back by nails - this is supposed to have given them greater grasp and sensitivity. Monkeys with full stereoscopic vision were supposed to have evolved by fifty million years ago, and the separation of the New World Monkeys from the Old World Monkeys is supposed to have occurred about fifteen million years later.

Over the next ten million years, it is thought that the early apes evolved, and that they lived in the tropical rain forests that evolutionists believe covered much of the Old World. These creatures were the dryopithecines: ape-like animals that moved on all fours as a monkey does. Evolutionists believe that as the forests began to shrink and gave way to more open woodland and grassland, some of the early apes evolved into creatures suitably adapted to the new open environment. It is believed that these creatures changed their diet to coarser foods and so their teeth changed - they developed relatively larger and thicker enamelled cheek teeth. Evolutionists believe that by fifteen million years ago, the ramapithecines had evolved and from these creatures the australopithecines developed some four million years ago.

According to evolutionists, the habilines, who are supposed to have lived about two million years ago, also evolved from the ramapithecines. Over the next half a million years, the brain size of these 'early primitive people' is supposed to have increased in size so that by one and a half million years ago, the *Homo erectus* people had evolved with a brain size that was double that of chimpanzees. The *Homo erectus* people are supposed to have continued to evolve until perhaps a hundred and fifty thousand years ago when early *Homo sapiens* people with a brain size of

Evolutionary views about the origin of people

Hydrogen is a colourless odourless gas, which if given enough time, turns into people...

'We are here as a result of a series of accidents, if you like. There was nothing preplanned about humanity.'

Richard Leakey in 'The Making of Mankind I', published in *The Listener*, (7 May 1981), p.598.

'This last chapter has been devoted to only one species, ourselves. This may have given the impression that somehow man is the ultimate triumph of evolution, that all these millions of years of development have had no purpose other than to put him on earth. There is no scientific evidence whatsoever to support such a view and no reason to suppose that our stay here will be any more permanent than that of the dinosaur.'

David Attenborough in the concluding remarks of *Life on Earth*, (Collins/BBC, 1979), p.308.

1300c.c., had been reached. Evolutionists teach that as the brain case expanded, the jaws receded to give modern people a flatter facial profile than their ancestors. The brain is not supposed to have grown uniformly - the greatest growth was supposed to be in the parietal and frontal lobes, which are important not only for muscle co-ordination, but also for the ability to concentrate on complex tasks and to plan ahead.

Evolutionists believe that by forty thousand years ago, *Homo sapiens sapiens* (i.e. modern humans) had evolved from the early *Homo sapiens* people. It is believed that the first modern people were hunter-gatherers, but that as time went on, they learnt first how to domesticate animals, then plants. This agricultural revolution, as it is called, is supposed to have occurred about ten thousand years ago and slowly to have altered people's whole way of life, for they began to live in settlements and then build bigger and bigger towns until real cities were built. Thus began the way of life that most of us live today.

As can be seen, these two accounts of origins are totally different from each another. In the Genesis account, we see that God was very prominent in our origins, whereas in the evolutionist's account there is no room for God's creativity, for everything in it is the result of chance natural processes. What I want us to do, however, is to look at what evidence there is for the evolutionary account of origins. First of all, let us look at the evidence of the fossils. What, if anything, do the fossils say about evolution?

3.
What about the fossil evidence?

In the last chapter we considered in some detail the evolutionary account of the origin of people. Now one of the purposes of this book is to look at the scientific evidence to see if it favours such an evolutionary account of human origins. It is not my intention, however, to repeat the critiques of the scientific evidence for an evolutionary origin of the universe and the solar system, as this has been given by others.[1] Although some of the unscientific aspects of the idea of chemical evolution are touched upon later in chapter 5, more detailed critiques of chemical evolution may be found elsewhere.[2]

I want us to begin our scientific quest by considering what, if anything, fossils teach about evolution. I realize that many people find palaeontology (that is, the study of fossils) to be a rather dull and boring subject, while others (myself included) find it a most invigorating and fascinating study. The fossils can reveal some very important answers to the questions that we have about origins, and so we must spend some time looking at them to see what facts we can discover. What I want us to do in this chapter is to consider what the fossil record teaches us about evolution in general, and about human origins in particular.

The fossil record

Before we look at this, I want us first to consider what we mean by the fossil record. Our English word, fossil, is from the Latin *fossilis* which means 'something dug up'. The present-day meaning of the word fossil is a relic or trace of past life preserved in the rocks. This can be a preserved hard part of the creature, such as a shell or a bone or a tooth; or it can be a trace made by the creature when it was alive, such as a footprint. All the fossils that are found in all the sedimentary rocks are regarded together as the fossil record.

Charles Darwin proposed the gradual evolution of life-forms over a long period of time. On this basis, you would expect to find this gradual evolution of the various life-forms recorded in fossilized form in the sedimentary rocks. However, it is true to say that the evolutionary account of the origin of species, in general, and of the origin of people, in particular, is not substantiated by the fossil record. Gish[3] and Hitching[4] have both written eloquent criticisms of evolution each from a different perspective: Gish as a creationist, and Hitching as an evolutionist. Both are agreed that the fossil record does not support the idea of the evolution of life on earth, as can be seen from the following quotations taken from their books. Gish states, 'We have cited example after example of failure to find transitional forms where evolutionary theory predicts such forms should have been found... The examples cited in this book are in no way exceptions but serve to illustrate what is characteristic of the fossil record.'[5]

Similarly Hitching states, 'Logically, then, the fossil record ought to show this stately progression. If we find fossils at all, and if Darwin's theory was right, we can predict what the rocks should contain: finely graduated fossils leading from one group of creatures to another group of creatures at a higher level of complexity. The minor "improvements" in successive generations should be as readily preserved as the species themselves. But this isn't so.'[6]

In other words, the intermediate transitional forms expected on the basis of slow gradual change of one kind of creature into another are not found fossilized in the sedimentary rocks.

Now the strange thing about this is that Darwin himself realized that the fossil record did not support the theory of evolution, for he wrote in his *Origin of Species* the following remarkable confession: 'The number of intermediate varieties which have formerly existed on earth must be truly enormous. Why then is not every geological formation and every stratum full of such intermediate links? Geology assuredly does not reveal any such finely graduated organic chain; and this, perhaps, is the most obvious and gravest objection which can be urged against my theory.'[7]

It is almost 130 years since Charles Darwin wrote these words and at the time he attributed this absence of transitional forms to the 'extreme imperfection' of the fossil record.[8] Since that time, however, literally millions of fossils have been found and examined, but still the transitional forms are absent, as Professor Derek Ager of University College Swansea pointed out to a critic of his presidential address to the Geologists' Association: 'We do *not* see lots and lots of species all gradually changing from bed to bed; what we do see is a species persisting through a certain thickness of strata and then suddenly being replaced by something else.'[9]

In other words, the fossil record does not show the continuous development of one kind of creature into another, but a series of creatures which are separated by gaps. That these gaps are real has been stated forcibly by the evolutionist Professor D. B. Kitts of the University of Oklahama: 'Despite the bright promise that palaeontology provides a means of "seeing" evolution, it has presented some nasty difficulties for evolutionists, the most notorious of which is the presence of "gaps" in the fossil record. Evolution requires intermediate forms between species and palaeontology does not provide them.'[10]

It cannot be overemphasized that there are many places in the fossil record where it is expected that plenty of intermediates should be found - yet they are just not there: 'The absence of connecting links is especially noticeable in the fossil record of the more peculiar kinds of animals. For example, the *cetacea* (whales, dolphins, and porpoises), *sirenia* (manatee, dugong, and sea cows), *pinnipedia* (sea lions, seals, and walruses), turtles, kangaroos, bats, dragon flies, spiders, and other types are isolated in the fossil record. In each such group the fossils are all distinguished by the peculiar features necessary for their separate classification. Their evolutionary origins are represented by missing links and speculations.'[11]

So why then do evolutionists continue to believe in evolution seeing that it is not substantiated in the fossil record? This is something we will try to answer in the next section.

Fossils and faith

To put it very simply, evolutionists believe in evolution because of their faith. It is not by observation, nor by experimentation, nor by scientific method, but it is by *faith* - faith in extrapolation, faith in natural processes operating over vast periods of time, faith in speculation and faith in missing links.

The evolutionists base many of their ideas on Hutton's catch-phrase, 'The present is the key to the past.' That is, natural geological processes which are observed to be in action at present, such as erosion, sedimentation, glaciation, vulcanism and so on - all operating in essentially the same fashion as at present - are invoked to explain the origin and formation of all the earth's geological deposits. This principle of uniformitarianism can never actually be *proved* to be valid, no matter how reasonable it seems. It should be noted, however, that the uniform and dependable operation of natural processes is the foundation of modern experimental science, without which modern science as we know it would be quite impossible. However, the science of geology, together with all the evolutionary ideas it envelops, is unique in that it deals with events that are past and are therefore non-repeatable. Here, the principle of uniformitarianism is assumed and hence by observing the present, the geologist/evolutionist extrapolates (or guesses) what has happened in the past.

That the evolutionist guesses at what has happened in the past has been confirmed by Professor W. R. Thompson FRS, Director of the Commonwealth Institute of Biological Research, Ottawa. He wrote the following in his introduction to the 1956 Everyman edition of *Origin of Species:* 'To establish the continuity required by Darwin's theory, historical arguments are invoked even though historical evidence is lacking. Thus are engendered those fragile towers of hypothesis based on hypothesis, where fact and fiction mingle in an inextricable confusion.'

It would appear therefore that much of evolution is not based on fact at all, but is rather *mountains of speculation without a molehill of fact.* That evolution is a great deal of speculation which has not been subjected to scientific method is illustrated by the following quotation taken from the book *Man Real and Ideal* written by the late Professor E. G. Conklin of Princeton: 'The concept of organic evolution is very highly prized by biologists, for whom it is an object of genuinely religious devotion, because they regard it as a supreme integrative principle. This is probably why severe methodological criticism employed in other departments of biology has not yet been brought to bear on evolutionary speculation.'[12]

That evolutionists have to exercise their faith in accounting for the evolution of life on earth was pointed out in a letter to *Science* in 1973 by E. C. Lucas, who at the time of writing was a self-confessed agnostic. He wrote that 'Evolutionists have to have faith in the original existence of the missing transitional forms.' And so they do, as we have already seen. The evolutionists' faith could be defined as '*the fossils hoped for, the evidence of missing links not seen*'.

The faith of the evolutionist is also confirmed by Professor L. H. Matthews in his introduction to the 1971 edition of Darwin's *Origin of Species*. He wrote, 'Most biologists accept it [that is, evolution] as though it were a proven fact, although this conviction rests upon circumstantial evidence. It forms a satisfactory faith on which to base our interpretation of nature.'

Again Professor Sidney Fox, one of the leading proponents of chemical evolution, wrote, 'Finally, I respond to friendly enquiries about a "faith" that kept one investigator on his research trail through many long years. That faith was a deep *conviction* that no other process could have resulted in the tremendous array of varied and variegated organisms...The *article of faith* is what is evolvable is solvable'[13] (emphasis added).

But the most remarkable statement about the faith of the evolutionist was made by the late Professor L. T. More of the University of Cincinnati when he penned the following confession in his book *The Dogma of Evolution:* 'Our faith in the idea of evolution depends upon our reluctance to accept the antagonistic doctrine of special creation.'

So it really boils down to the fact that people prefer to believe in evolution than to believe in a creation by an almighty God.

The origin of animals

We have already seen that in general terms the fossil record does not provide the transitional forms required by evolution. But is this true when we look at specific types of creatures? What I want us to do in this section is to see what we can learn from the fossil record about the origins of the animals, and in particular I want us to look at the origins of fishes, amphibians, reptiles and mammals.

Before we look at the vertebrates (that is, animals with backbones, such as the fishes, the amphibians, the reptiles and the mammals), we must first look at the invertebrates (that is, animals without backbones). The evolutionist calls the oldest rocks on the earth the Precambrian rocks. It is in these rocks that we should find evidence of multicellular organisms evolving into the invertebrates. Interestingly enough, very few fossil remains have been found in the Precambrian rocks, and those that have been found are either the remains of the blue-green algae, or complex invertebrates similar to those found in the Cambrian rocks. No forerunners of these complex invertebrates have been found.

In the Cambrian rocks, we find millions of fossils of invertebrate animals - sponges, corals, clams, snails, crabs, sea-urchins, jelly fish, the extinct trilobites, as well as the extinct graptolites. These animals are all very complex and complicated, yet nowhere do we find a record of their evolution. Daniel Axelrod has described this as 'one of the major unsolved problems of geology and evolution', and in the same article goes on to remind us that 'When we turn to examine the Precambrian rocks for the forerunners of these Early Cambrian fossils, they are nowhere to be found. Many thick (over 5,000 feet) sections of sedimentary rock are known to lie in unbroken succession below strata containing the earliest Cambrian fossils. These sediments apparently were suitable for the preservation of fossils because they are often identical with overlying rocks which are fossiliferous, yet no fossils are found in them.'[14]

This sudden appearance of invertebrates in the Cambrian rocks is recognized by the evolutionist and poses a major problem, for when we look at the fossils in the Precambrian rocks, we do not find animals which are evolving into trilobites, for instance, or into any other invertebrate animal, for that matter. This is strange, for we should expect this if evolution has occurred.

A similar sort of situation is found when we examine the fossil record for the evolution of the invertebrates into the vertebrates. The evolution from invertebrate to vertebrate would supposedly have passed through a state where the animal possessed a rod-like notochord, but the fossil record does not provide us with any such creature: 'How this earliest chordate stock evolved, what stages of development it went through to eventually give rise to truly fishlike creatures, we do not know. Between the Cambrian, when it probably originated, and the Ordovician, when the first fossils of animals with really fishlike characteristics appeared, there is a gap of perhaps 100 million years which we will probably never be able to fill.'[15]

Although this was written in 1964, the situation is still the same, for in 1985, after reviewing the situation with respect to the knowledge of the evolution of fishes at that time, Dr Duane Gish concluded, 'The fossil record has thus not produced ancestors nor transitional forms for the major fish classes. Such hypothetical ancestors and the required transitional forms must, on the basis of the known record, be merely the products of speculation.'[16]

We can see therefore that there is no proof in the fossil record that the vertebrates evolved from the invertebrates, or from anything else for that matter.

The evolution of the fish into the amphibian is not found in the fossil record. Fishes are found; amphibians are found; fisho-amphibians (or should they be called amphibio-fishes?) are not found. The rock strata have been searched in vain for a series of fossils showing the evolution of a fish into an amphibian. For example, not a single transitional form has ever been found showing an intermediate stage between the fin of a fish and the limb of an amphibian. On the basis of evolution you should expect to find numerous transitional forms for this one transformation alone, but the fossil record is strangely silent in telling us anything about it.

It was once thought that the lobed-finned fish were candidates for the link between the fish and the amphibians. These fish were thought to have used their bony fins to crawl out of the water to live part of their life on land. It was thought that they eventually evolved into amphibians and so became extinct. However, one of these lobed-finned fish was spotted by the naturalist Majorie Courtenay-Latimer in a trawler's catch at the South African port of East London in December 1938. Realizing that it was no ordinary fish, she sent a sketch of it to Professor J. L. B. Smith, an ichthyologist at Rhodes University in Grahamstown, South Africa. He identified it as a Coelacanth, a fish that was supposed to have become extinct about sixty million years ago. Since 1938, over a hundred other Coelacanths have been caught and recently they have been photographed swimming in their natural habitat.[17] These remarkable photographs show that the Coelacanth is100% fish and lives at a depth of 170-200 metres off the west coast of Grande Comore island in the Indian Ocean. They use their bony fins not for crawling out onto the land, but in a well-co-ordinated fashion for swimming around in the depths of the ocean. It appears that they are unable to use them even to walk on the sea bottom, and they certainly do not crawl out of the sea! The discovery of the Coelacanth and observation of its way of life has ruled out the possibility of the lobed-finned fish as a link between the fish and the amphibians.

We saw in chapter 2 that the evolutionist teaches that amphibians evolved into reptiles and that reptiles then evolved into mammals. However, the fossil record does not support this idea, as we shall see. The animal *Seymouria,* which is said to be transitional between amphibians and reptiles, is found in the Permian rocks. However, the true reptile *Hylonomus* (from the order Cotylosauria) is found in Pennsylvanian rocks and the problem is that these rocks are dated twenty million years *older* than the Permian rocks. So the question is: how could *Seymouria,* the ancestor of the reptile *Hylonomus,* live twenty million years *after* the reptile *Hylonomus* lived? It is just impossible! Furthermore, the so-called mammal-like reptiles of the subclass Synapsida, which are supposed to be the ancestors of the mammals, are also found in Pennsylvanian rocks. This means that *Seymouria* (found in the Permian rocks, remember) would not only postdate the reptiles by some twenty million years, but would also postdate the supposed ancestors of the mammals by an equal period of time!

It is this evolutionary time sequence which gives rise to one of the major problems with respect to the proposed evolution of mammals. As Dr Duane Gish points out, 'In order for the facts of the fossil record to fit the predictions of the evolution model, a true time-sequence must be established that accords with these predictions.'[18] This means that an evolutionary series of animals must be found in the correct evolutionary date order in the rocks. We have already seen in the last paragraph that this is not the case for the amphibian-reptile-mammal transition.

Another major problem in the supposed evolution of the mammals is the change from a reptilian-like jaw to a mammal-like jaw. Dr Duane Gish sums up the problem as follows: 'In mammals there is a single bone in each half of the lower jaw, called the dentary, since it bears the teeth, and this bone articulates directly with the squamosal area of the skull. Reptiles have six bones in each half of the lower jaw. Articulation of the jaw with the skull is indirect, with the articular [one of the bones of the jaw] articulating with the quadrate bone, a bone not found in mammals. Another fundamental difference between reptiles and mammals is the fact that all reptiles, living or fossil, have a single bone in the ear, a rod-like bone known as the columella. Mammals possess three bones in the ear, the stapes, malleus and incus. Evolutionists maintain that the stapes corresponds to the columella and that the quadrate and articular bones of the reptile somehow moved into the ear to become, respectively, the incus and malleus bones of the mammalian ear. No explanation is given how the intermediates managed to hear while this was going on.'[19]

Thousands of fossil reptiles have been found and these all possess a single ear bone and multiple jaw bones. Thousands of fossil mammals have been found and these all possess three ear bones and a single bone in the jaw. Not a single fossil has been found that represents an intermediate stage - one that has two ear bones and three jaw bones, for example.

Not only is the rise and development of the mammals in general not documented in the fossil record, but neither is that of particular groups of mammals. For example, the fossil record does not detail the evolution of the rodents (order Rodentia) as pointed out by Romer in his classic *Vertebrate Paleontology:* 'The origin of the rodents is obscure. When they first appear, in the late Paleocene, in the genus *Paramys,* we are already dealing with a typical, if rather primitive, true rodent, with the definitive ordinal characters well developed. Presumably, of course, they had arisen from some basal, insectivorous, placental stock, but no transitional forms are known.'[20]

Neither does the fossil record give any information about the evolution of the sea-dwelling mammals (order Cetacea). In spite of the claims made by evolutionists that the whales have evolved from terrestrial mammals, the *Encyclopaedia Britannica* contains the following remarkable admission: 'The earliest known fossils are perfectly good whales and clearly assignable to one of the three groups (i.e. Archaeoceti, Odontoceti or Mysticeti); thus there is no concrete evidence linking the three nor is there evidence as to their ancestry.'[21]

Nor does the fossil record give any information about the origin of flying mammals such as the bats (order Chiroptera), or indeed of any other group of mammals you may wish to name.

Although reptiles and mammals can be distinguished on the basis of skeletal features, it is much easier to distinguish them by their soft parts, for example, mode of reproduction, warm-bloodedness, mode of breathing due to possession of a diaphragm, suckling of the young, and possession of hair. The evolution of such structures are usually portrayed in 'abracadabra'-type stories, such as in the following: 'The animals changed too. Some of the reptiles in the colder regions began to develop a method of keeping their bodies warm. Their heat output increased when it was cold and their heat loss was cut down when scales became smaller and more pointed, and evolved into fur. Sweating was also an adaptation to regulate the body temperature, a device to cool the body when necessary by evaporation of water. But incidentally the young of these reptiles began to lick the sweat of the mother for nourishment. Certain sweat glands began to secrete a richer and richer secretion, which eventually became milk. Thus the young of these early mammals had a better start in life.'[22] There is not one iota of proof in the fossil record for such a story. Again it is no more than mountains of speculation, and, incidentally, there is not a molehill of fact to substantiate it.

The origin of people

Charles Darwin caused quite a stir when he suggested that humans are closely related to the apes; in other words that a human being was an animal - a special animal, no doubt; an intelligent animal, no doubt; but an animal nevertheless. Up to that time, it was generally believed that humans were very special creatures that had nothing in common with the animal world. Evolutionists now insist that humans are animals and that they are members of a group of mammals known as the primates. As the primates include monkeys and apes, the evolutionists believe that humans, monkeys and apes have all descended from a common ancestor.

Now the crucial question that we need to ask is 'Is this what the fossil record teaches?' We have not got the time to go into great detail about the various fossil finds that have been found and that are purported to link humans with the apes. Even if we did, I am sure that we might be in danger of not seeing the wood for the trees, so to speak. What I want us to do therefore is to look at the fossil record and see what the overall picture is. Those who want more detail are directed elsewhere.[23]

Now one of the problems of discussing the significance, or otherwise, of our fossil ancestors is that there is little evidence to go on: 'The material mainly consists of bone fragments and teeth, rarely complete skulls or jaws - and no complete skeletons at all.'[24]

The paucity of actual evidence has evoked the following statement from Richard Leakey: 'David Pilbeam comments wryly, "If you brought in a smart scientist from another discipline and showed him the meagre evidence we've got he'd surely say, 'Forget it; there isn't enough to go on'." Neither David nor others involved in the search for mankind can take this advice, of course, but we remain fully aware of the dangers of drawing conclusions from evidence that is so incomplete.'[25]

This is one of the reasons that I intend to go rather quickly through this particular section. Furthermore, the arguments and counter-arguments change very quickly, so I am endeavouring just to give the jist of the arguments that I hope will remain valid for a number of years.

We have already seen that in general the fossil record is full of gaps. This is exactly the same picture that we find when we look at the supposed evolution of the primates. The primates are supposed to have evolved from an insectivorous ancestor, but as usual there is no series of intermediate forms showing such a transition: 'The transition from insectivore to primate is not documented by fossils. The basis of knowledge about the transition is by inference from living forms.'[26]

Hence even if we consider humans to belong to the order of primates, we can see at the very outset that there is no evidence in the fossil record for the evolution of the entire primate order! The primates, as a group, are therefore completely isolated from all other animals.

Now according to the evolutionists, the first primates were the prosimians, and these are supposed to have evolved into the Platyrrhines (these are the New World Monkeys, with their

flattened noses and their sideways pointing nostrils) and also into
the Catarrhines (these include the Old World Monkeys, apes and
humans, all of whom have nostrils that point downwards). There
is no evidence in the fossil record for such evolution: no transitional
forms have been found that link the prosimians with the
Platyrrhines; and no transitional forms have been found that link
the prosimians with the Catarrhines.

Within the Catarrhines, humans and apes are placed in the
superfamily *hominoidea* by the evolutionary scientist. This superfamily includes the gibbon, the gorilla, the chimpanzee, the orang-
utan and humans. Such creatures are called hominoids, and
according to the evolutionist, an ape-like ancestral hominoid gave
rise to the gorilla and another which split again to give rise to the
chimpanzee and humans. It cannot be overemphasized, however,
that the assumed ancestor of apes and humans has never been found
and its existence is purely hypothetical, in spite of what is written
in popular evolutionary books. The evolutionists cannot even
identify our supposed ancestral hominoid, as the following recent
quotation shows: 'Candidates for intermediate ancestors that have
been proposed include two from Kenya known as *Proconsul* and
Kenyapithecus; two from India, Pakistan, China, and Kenya called
Ramapithecus and *Sivapithecus;* and two from Europe called
Rudapithecus and *Dryopithecus*... Despite much debate and speculation, none of these primates has been finally accepted as a human
progenitor.'[27]

In other words, there is no transitional form linking humans
with an animal ancestor. No more really needs to be said! There
is no evidence from the fossil record linking humans to their
supposed animal ancestors.

Yet in spite of this, claims are made by evolutionists that
humans have evolved from ape-like ancestors. One claim is that
humans are descended from the australopithecines. (The australopithecines are supposed to have descended from the so-called early
apes, but again there is no evidence of this transition in the fossil
record.) There are several species of australopithecines, the most
famous being *Australopithecus afarensis,* and it is from this species
of australopithecine that evolutionists maintain that humans have
descended. The most famous fossil member of this species was
discovered in 1974 in the Afar Triangle of Ethiopia by Don
Johanson of the Cleveland Museum. She was named 'Lucy' after

the Beatles' song 'Lucy in the Sky with Diamonds' which was being played on a tape recorder by Don Johanson and his colleagues at their campsite on the evening of her discovery. Lucy was hailed by Don Johanson as being our ancestor and was at first upheld as being the proverbial missing link. The evidence against Lucy being an ape-woman linking humans with the animal kingdom is, however, very powerful,[28] and in the opinion of many evolutionists, Lucy is now considered to be no more than an arboreal ape, similar to all the other australopithecines.

The creatures that I want us to look at next are called *Homo habilis*, which means 'handy man'; they are also called the habilines. Some evolutionists maintain that the habilines descended from the australopithecines, while others argue that they descended from the ramapithecines. There is, however, no evidence in the fossil record to support either view. In fact, australopithecines and habilines are found in the same rock strata, showing that they lived at the same time and that the one could not be the ancestor of the other. The name *Homo habilis* was originally given to some fossils that were found at Olduvai in East Africa from 1959 onwards. Since then, more fossils have been found that have been assigned as belonging to the habilines. However, some evolutionists have suggested that not all the fossils that have been assigned to the habiline group actually belong to it - they maintain that some are australopithecines.[29] If we removed these australopithecines from the habiline group, then we would be left with what we might call the true habilines - and it is these true habilines that I want us to consider.

Now one of the questions that we must ask about the true habilines is: were they human? The varied stone tool kits that are found associated with the habiline finds would appear to indicate that they had *intelligence*. However, brain casts of the habilines' skulls show that they did not possess a very large brain - about half the average size of that of a modern human. But the habilines were much smaller than modern humans. From the size of their bones, it can be estimated that they probably weighed only about forty kilograms - about the same as a twelve-year-old child. So, for their size, the habilines had fairly large brains. Furthermore, casts made of habilines' brains show them to be in the modern human pattern with a bulge in the Broca's area - the region essential for speech.[30]

So it would appear that there are valid reasons for believing that the true habilines were human.

Most evolutionists now concede that the fossil form called *Homo erectus* is a human with what they call 'primitive' features - these people had protruding jaws, no chin, thick brow ridges and a long low skull (a bit like a partially deflated football). The fossilized remains of the *Homo erectus* people have been found in East, South and North Africa, as well as in Asia (India, China, and countries in South East Asia). The characteristic hand axes of the *Homo erectus* people have been found in Europe, but very few remains: 'A handful of specimens, such as the Arago remains excavated by Henry and Marie-Antoinette de Lumley in the Pyrenees foothills of France, the huge Heidelberg jaw from Germany, and the back of a skull from Vértesszöllös, Hungary, are sometimes called *erectus*. A number of authorities, however, regard them as early, or archaic, forms of *Homo sapiens*.'[31]

The *Homo erectus* people are supposed to have evolved from the habilines, although again such a transition is not substantiated in the fossil record. Furthermore, remains of the habilines and *Homo erectus* people have been found in rocks dated as being of the same age, which shows that they lived at the same time and so that one could not be the ancestor of the other.

Although they had a brain size of about 1000 ml., compared with the average of 1350 ml. for the modern European, the *Homo erectus* people were certainly intelligent. For example, they were able to control fire so that they could cook their food. They also made very elegant double-edged, teardrop-shaped 'hand axes' (at least that is what they are called, although no one really knows just how they were used). This indicates that these people used their brains in a similar way to that in which we use ours: they had the ability to conceive a design for a stone tool and to work a piece of stone until that design was achieved. This is known as conceptualized thinking and, according to linguists, this is the type of thinking that we do when we speak a language. This is one piece of evidence that can be used to show that these people spoke. Another piece of evidence comes by comparing the position of the tongue and larynx - this also indicates that the *Homo erectus* people were capable of speech.

Some evolutionists suggest that the *Homo erectus* people were a small form of Neanderthal Man and so *Homo erectus* and *Homo sapiens* would be one and the same species.[32] Interestingly, the fossil skull from Petralona in Greece has a mixture of *Homo erectus* and *Homo sapiens* characteristics. There are those evolutionists who argue that this is an example of a transition from *Homo erectus* to *Homo sapiens*.[33] However, fossilized *Homo erectus* skulls which post-date *Homo sapiens* have been found in Australia,[34] showing that the one could not have evolved into the other. Other anthropologists see variations such as the Petralona skull as proving that the *Homo erectus* people were an early form of our own species.[35] Adding strength to such an argument is the recent discovery of the fossilized skeleton of a twelve-year-old *Homo erectus* boy near Lake Turkana, Kenya. The post-cranial skeleton differs only subtly from that of a modern child. An article about him concludes: 'Suitably clothed and with a cap to obscure his low forehead and beetle brow, he would probably go unnoticed in a crowd today.'[36]

At present, therefore, the evolutionists seem to be arguing that *Homo erectus* is a misnomer and that these people should be reclassified as *Homo sapiens*.

We will learn more about the Neanderthals in the next chapter. All that need concern us now is that these people lived in Europe and in the Middle East. From several sites in France, where remains of Neanderthal people have been found, we learn that they built shelters of saplings covered with animal skins, within the mouths of caves. They also used animal skins for clothing - by sewing them together. They cooked their food on fires, even using stone hot plates. There is also evidence that they attempted writing.[37]

Perhaps the most significant evidence of Neanderthal life is the way they dealt with death - they conducted funerals and held ritual burials complete with grave goods, including tools and food. Bodies found in some of their graves were surrounded by skulls of ibex, a species of wild goat. One grave in Iraq even had clusters of pollen grains that have been identified as the remains of flowers, all but one of which are known today to have medicinal properties. All this would suggest that the Neanderthals were beings with a sense of the spiritual.

About ten Neanderthals, six of them fairly complete skeletons, have been found in a cemetery in the Skuhl Cave on Mount Carmel. These fossils were modern, but with a wide range of Neanderthal characteristics - some were not unlike those of the fossil remains of a woman found in the adjacent Tabun Cave. This has led some anthropologists to suggest that the Neanderthal people and modern people lived together and intermarried (just as people of different races intermarry today), although this has been disputed by others. Other Neanderthals dug out of a cave at Shanidar in the mountains of northern Iraq show the same characteristics as those from Mount Carmel. In another cave at Qafzeh near Nazareth Neanderthals have been found that do not look like the classical Neanderthaler, but in many ways they are similar to the Cro Magnon people of Europe and Western Asia.

Cro Magnon people were truly modern people. They are probably best remembered for their art - they carved bone and ivory representations of the animals and people around them and they painted on cave walls, such as those at Lascaux, examples of the living animals, so that we know exactly what the woolly mammoth and rhinoceros looked like. The Cro Magnon peoples that populated the European plains in what is now the Ukraine were mammoth hunters, and they built their homes of mammoth bones covered with skins, and they dressed in clothing made of hare skins. In 1981 it was discovered that they had constructed a set of musical instruments from mammoth bones.[38] Cro Magnon people are only a cultural step away from people who live in the microchip space age in the latter part of the twentieth century.

At the end of this rather lengthy section, we are forced to the conclusion that there is no evidence from the fossil record linking humans to animals. Creatures, such as the australopithecines, which were once thought by evolutionists to be human-like are now considered to be completely ape. Other creatures, such as the *Homo erectus* people, which were once thought by evolutionists to be ape-like, are now considered to be completely human. There is no evidence in the fossil record that ape-people have ever existed.

Explanations of the gaps

We have seen clearly that the transitional forms predicted by evolution are not found in the fossil record. Although the fossil record is literally teeming with millions of fossils, yet at the same time it could be said that the fossil record is also full of gaps. How does the evolutionist explain away the gaps in the fossil record?

What I want us to do in this section is to consider three of the most popularly accepted explanations given by evolutionists for the absence of fossilized transitional forms.

In the first explanation, it is assumed that at least a hundred times more fossil species have lived than have been discovered in the fossil record.[39] It is then argued that we do not find transitional forms in the fossil record because these transitional forms are in the 99% of the species that are not discovered in the fossil record. This is a ridiculous line of reasoning, for it starts by assuming that evolution has occurred and inherent in this assumption is the idea that transitional forms must have existed. It is then concluded that transitional forms have existed and therefore that evolution has occurred!

In the second explanation, a pattern for evolution is proposed which makes it unlikely that any intermediate forms will be fossilized. This model has been proposed by Professor Ernst Mayr[40] and is called 'allopatric speciation' - in other words that new species are formed 'in another place'. According to this theory for example, a new mountain range would cause a small portion of the population of a particular animal to become isolated. It is then suggested that evolution would occur more rapidly in this cut-off portion as natural selection operated more intensively. Within a relatively short period of time, a new and more powerful species would have developed. This better species would then spread back into its former territory (the mountain range presumably having been eroded away in the meantime) and quickly conquer it. Because the chances of finding fossils in the cut-off population while it was evolving are rare, it is argued that intermediate forms would not be found.

Although such an argument sounds convincing enough on paper, again it is based on the assumption that evolution occurs, which has yet to be demonstrated. It is known that *horizontal* differentiation can occur so that, for example, one species of gull may develop into another species of gull because of geographical separation (as in the case of the herring gull/lesser black backed gull). But it has not been demonstrated that *vertical* differentiation occurs - an example of this would be the change of a fish into an amphibian. Here the differences between the two types of animal are great in that they have different modes of locomotion, breathing, breeding and so on. Furthermore, it has not been demonstrated that there is any connection between horizontal and vertical differentiation.

Again, as in the first example, it has been assumed that evolution has occurred and this is then used as *proof* that the intermediate forms existed 'in another place', even though there is not one shred of evidence that such transitional forms ever existed. The unproven existence of the intermediate forms is therefore used as proof that evolution has occurred.

The third and most recent explanation of the non-existence of transitional forms in the fossil record is that which has been put forward by Niles Eldredge of the American Museum of Natural History and Stephen J. Gould, Professor of Geology at Harvard. Since the early 1970s, they have been proposing that evolution is not gradual and of constant tempo, but that the evidence from the fossil record is that 'There are short periods of rapid change at speciation, separated by longer periods in which there is no change.'[41] Professor Ager describes it as being 'like the life of a soldier, [which] consists of long periods of boredom and short periods of terror'.[42]

Eldredge and Gould have called this the 'punctuated equilibrium' model of evolution, and according to this model, '(1) The intermediates between species existed in small populations, and small populations are less likely to leave a record than large ones; (2) evolution is rapid in the small isolated population, and (3) the intermediates did not exist in the same place as [and so are unlikely to be preserved with] their ancestor.'[43]

Naturally, this model has received a fair amount of criticism by other evolutionists.[44] One of these areas is that of natural selection because punctuated equilibrium evolution challenges this sacred cow of evolution. In the punctuated equilibrium model, natural selection operates on the micro level to tune things up a bit, but it has nothing to do with the big question: the origin of new types and kinds. This is what creationists have been saying for years.

Another major criticism of the punctuated equilibrium idea of evolution is that in this model it is proposed that evolution is rapid and occurs in small isolated populations. For example, it is argued that most species arose within hundreds or thousands of years. This is in total contrast with the orthodox view that species evolved very slowly through very large numbers of very small changes. Furthermore, we do not see this type of evolution occurring today. If species are supposed to have evolved quickly in hundreds of years, such evolution would be observable - but no such observations are recorded.

So the evolutionist really has no explanation for the missing transitional forms in the fossil record. The missing links are still missing; that is why they are called 'missing'. The evolutionist will not accept the inevitable and admit that evolution has not occurred. Instead he produces all types of weird and wonderful explanations in order to explain away one of the most damning pieces of evidence against the idea of the evolution of life on earth - the fact that there are no transitional forms in the fossil record.

Conclusion

In this chapter we have looked at the fossil record to see what, if anything, this teaches us about our origins. We have seen that the idea that humans are the result of an evolutionary process is not substantiated by the fossils that are found in the sedimentary rocks on the earth. We saw that the fossil record is full of gaps. By this we mean that intermediate forms, linking one type of animal to another, are not found in the fossil record. For example, apes are found in the fossil record; people are found in the fossil record; but ape-people, linking humans to the apes, are not found in the fossil record. The missing link is still missing!

We also looked at the explanations that are given for the gaps in the fossil record and saw that none of these stands up to scientific investigation.

Yet in spite of the fact that the fossil record shouts a resounding 'No!' to the idea that evolution has occurred, evolutionists continue to believe in evolution; and this is because of their faith. We had a look at the evolutionists' faith and saw that this was real - what is often presented as fact is really nothing more than guesswork based on faith in evolution. Richard Leakey and Roger Lewin frankly admit that what the evolutionists guess about human origins is a matter of faith.[45] The rational scientist is not so rational after all! We saw that one evolutionist has made the remarkable admission that the reason for his faith in evolution was because he did not like the alternative of special creation. This should make us wonder how many other evolutionary scientists are like him.

Before we leave the fossil record, I want us to look at the reconstructions of ape-people and fossil people. Why are ape-people reconstructed if no such creatures have ever been found? How accurate are the reconstructions of fossil people? These are some of the questions I want us to consider in the next chapter which pointedly asks the question: 'Figments of the imagination?'

4.
Figments of the imagination?

We saw in the last chapter that there is no evidence from the fossils found in the sedimentary rocks of the earth that humans have evolved from ape-like ancestors. So why do we see so many drawings of ape-people in books written about our origins? Why are our natural history museums literally full of drawings and models of ape-people? Children (and their parents) confronted with such half-ape/half-human reconstructions are often convinced that there must be proof that such creatures existed. And in turn they believe that there must be proof that people are descended from ape-like ancestors. However, if ape-people never existed, how can we explain the existence of such depictions? Why do we see drawings and models of them? I hope to show you in this chapter that such reconstructions are no more than the figments of the human imagination.

Anthro art

Anthro art is the name given to the science of reconstructing a man or a woman from fossilized remains. First of all let us consider how an animal that has been fossilized is reconstructed. The scars on the fossilized bones show where muscles were once attached. By studying these and by comparing them with the bones and muscles of living creatures, it is possible to build up a picture of the creature's body and work out what each part could do. All this sounds relatively simple, but how accurate are such reconstructions? The simple answer to this question is: 'It depends'.

More often than not the reconstruction is based on preconceived ideas. For example, when dinosaurs were first reconstructed, it was assumed that because they were reptiles they would have a typical reptilian shape similar to that of the crocodile. The first fossilized dinosaurs that were found were therefore reconstructed with their legs sticking out of their sides, just like a crocodile. The Iguanodon, the first dinosaur to be discovered, was not only made to look like a crocodile, but was also given a nose horn. It was not until several skeletons of Iguanodon were found fossilized together in a Belgian coal mine that their true shape and form were realized and they were reconstructed accordingly. Far from resembling a crocodile, the Iguanodon stood on massive hind legs, had an enormous powerful tail, and would have reached out with its 'hands' to grasp the food it fed upon. It was also realized that the Iguanodon did not have a nose horn at all; the bony spike that had been used to construct the nose horn turned out to be a spike on the Iguanodon's thumbs!

Anyone who knew an elephant only by its skeleton would never guess that the creature had its nostrils at the tip of a long flexible trunk which also serves as a muscular fifth limb. Neither would they know anything about the size and shape of its ears, nor for that matter the colour of its skin. Similarly, the bones of fossil people tell us nothing about the fleshy parts of the nose, lips or ears. Skin colours, as well as hairiness, are also largely conjecture.

So, do not be fooled by drawings or models of ape-people. One of the first things to remember is that such reconstructions are very often made from one or two fragments of bone and are no more than the figments of preconceived ideas. This can be illustrated by considering the story of Java Man, who was discovered by Eugene Dubois, a former student of Professor Ernst Haeckel. We will learn more about Professor Haeckel in the next chapter; all that need concern us at present is that Professor Haeckel was so convinced that ape-people existed that he commissioned a drawing of such a creature, even though there was *no* tangible evidence for its existence whatsoever! He even gave this hypothetical creature the generic name *Pithecanthropus alanthus,* which means the ape-man without speech.

Indoctrinated with the preconceived ideas of his former professor, the young Dutch doctor Dubois went to the Far East in 1887 determined to find this hypothetical ape-man. Eventually he was convinced that he had found what he was looking for at Trinil on the island of Java. There, he found a couple of molar teeth, the broken cap of a skull, a human leg-bone and several leg-bone fragments. He called his find *Pithecanthropus erectus* and Professor Haeckel commissioned a life-size model of him to be constructed so that Java Man (as he was commonly called) could be exhibited in museums throughout Europe. However, we do well to remember what G. K. Chesterton wrote about such depictions of Java Man: 'Popular histories published portraits of him like the portraits of Charles I or George IV. A detailed drawing was reproduced carefully shaded to show the very hairs of his head were all numbered. No uninformed person, looking at its carefully lined face, would imagine for a moment that this was the portrait of a thigh bone, of a few teeth and a fragment of a cranium.'[1]

Furthermore, what Dubois had not told everybody was that he had found the bones and teeth in separate places and there was no reason at all to believe that they had come from the same individual. The only reason that he believed that they were from the same individual was that he was convinced that he would find an ape-man in the Far East and he made sure he appeared to do so, irrespective of what he actually found.

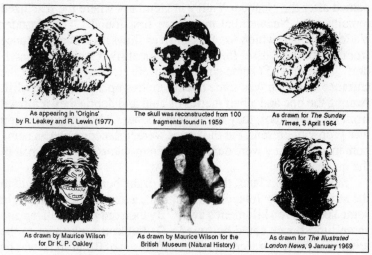

| As appearing in 'Origins' by R. Leakey and R. Lewin (1977) | The skull was reconstructed from 100 fragments found in 1959 | As drawn for *The Sunday Times*, 5 April 1964 |
| As drawn by Maurice Wilson for Dr K. P. Oakley | As drawn by Maurice Wilson for the British Museum (Natural History) | As drawn for *The Illustrated London News*, 9 January 1969 |

Artistic reconstruction of Zinjanthropus boisei

I hope that you will be beginning to realize that when an artist is drawing the outward appearance of a fossil - be it an ape, a human or any other creature for that matter - the drawing is the product of the artist's imagination and often reflects the preconceived ideas of that artist. This may be illustrated by considering the five different artistic impressions of *Zinjanthropus boisei* (see illustration). Those artists that wished this creature to be ape-like made him so, while those wanting him to appear man-like made him so. Interestingly, Maurice Wilson made him look ape-like for Dr Oakley and man-like for the British Museum! *Zinjanthropus boisei* is now classified as an australopithecine, which, as we have seen, were nothing more than arboreal apes! So much then for artistic impressions of this creature!

The Neanderthals

I want us now to turn our attention to one or two specific examples of where ape-like reconstructions from bones and/or teeth have have been found to be totally inaccurate. The first example is the early depictions of Neanderthals. The Neanderthal people are named after the Neander Valley in Germany where the fossilized remains of a Neanderthal man were first found. The Neander Valley, through which the Düssel river flows, is a short distance from where the Düssel flows into the great river Rhine at Düsseldorf. There in 1857 some quarrymen were clearing out a cave, the entrance of which was some twenty metres up a precipitous cliff. Among the one and a half metres of mud and debris they removed from the cave floor, they found some bones. The whole skeleton was probably present, but the bones were not recognized as being human and so they were dumped unceremoniously with the rest of the quarry debris.

Several weeks later, the existence of the bones was brought to the attention of Dr Johann Carl Fuhlrott, a teacher from Elberfeld some six to seven kilometres away. By then only the skullcap and some limb bones could be found. Dr Fuhlrott took them to the anatomist Professor Hermann Schaaffhausen of Bonn and it was he who presented Neanderthal Man, as he was then called, to the world. Since that time remains of other Neanderthal people have been discovered in other parts of Europe, and in North Africa and Asia.

Even today, the average conception of the Neanderthals is that they were shambling frowning brutes of low intelligence. This conception is one that was put forward originally and was perpetuated for about a hundred years. When first discovered, Neanderthal Man was considered to be a link between apes and humans. Consequently he was depicted as having divergent toes, like the apes, and as walking on the outer edges of his feet, like an orangutan. It was said that he could not straighten his knees and that he lacked the convex spine essential for upright posture. His head, with its heavy overhanging eyebrow ridges, its retreating forehead and its jutting jaw was depicted as being slung forward just like a gorilla. His face was given large eye sockets, a broad nose and a receding chin. All this was done to emphasize the ape-like appearance of this creature because it was firmly believed that the Neanderthals were half-ape/half-human.

It was not until the 1950s that the scientific community realized that many of the preconceived ideas about the Neanderthals were false. It was concluded that the curved limb bones of the skeleton from La Chapelle-aux-Saints was due to rickets and that the individual's stooped skeletal structure was due to arthritis (just as the anti-evolutionists had been saying for a long time). Two anatomists pointed out that the reconstruction of this particular individual was such that the centre of gravity was so far forward that he would have fallen flat on his face before even taking a step![2] They also concluded that there was 'no valid reason for assuming that the posture of Neanderthal Man differed significantly from that of present day man' and they went on to say that if he were bathed, shaved and dressed in modern clothing he would have passed unnoticed in a New York subway. It was at this time that the Neanderthals were placed in the same species as modern-day humans, and were put into the sub-species *Homo sapiens neanderthalensis.*

Nebraska Man

The story of Neanderthal Man is bad enough, but that of Nebraska

Man is much worse. I have related the following story publicly on many occasions, and I have often been challenged about its veracity by those who find it to be beyond belief. Some may find it difficult to believe that the following events actually took place, but I can assure you that they really did.

In 1922, an amateur geologist by the name of Harold J. Cook found a fossil tooth in the Snake Creek fossil beds in the Pliocene deposits in the American state of Nebraska. Thinking that it might be of some significance, he sent it to the famous Henry Fairfield Osborn, who was then head of the American Museum of Natural History. He believed that he could see that the tooth had human, chimpanzee and ape-man characteristics, and so he called the creature from whom the tooth had come, *Hesperopithecus haroldcooki*, which means 'Harold Cook's ape-man from the land where the sun sets'. There was great excitement about this find for now the Americans could boast that humans had evolved from the apes in the United States of America. This was an event that the American anthropologists had been anticipating for some time. Osborn was overjoyed and is quoted as declaring that 'This little tooth speaks volumes of truth, in that it affords evidence of man's descent from the ape.'[3]

Osborn's views were fully supported by the eminent anatomist Professor Sir Grafton Elliot Smith of the University of Manchester. He had a painting of Nebraska Man (and his wife) commissioned and this appeared in the *Illustrated London News* on 24 June 1922. As can be seen, the illustration showed Mr and Mrs Hesperopithecus at home in exotic prehistoric surroundings complete with prehistoric horses and camels nearby.

Nebraska Man was used in the famous Tennessee monkey trial in 1925 in order to prove that there was evidence that humans had descended from ape-like ancestors. In this trial, a teacher by the name of John Scopes was accused of teaching evolution, which was contrary to Tennessee state law. The *Hesperopithecus* tooth was used as evidence of human evolution. Although Scopes was found guilty, the trial marked a turning point in US education history. Hitherto, many states had laws forbidding the teaching of evolution, but from that time, such laws were revoked until eventually the evolutionary account of origins was taught in all state schools (called 'public schools') in the USA.

Some years after the Scopes trial, however, a Mr Thompson of the American Museum of Natural History returned to the place where Harold Cook had found the *Hesperopithecus* tooth. He found several similar teeth and was able to establish that the animal from which the original tooth had come was not ape-like at all. Nor was it human. In fact it was an extinct pig! This pig's tooth not only snapped at the preconceived ideas of the evolutionists, but it also bit the American education system, which until that time had not permitted the teaching of evolution in many of its schools. Its tooth mark is unfortunately still being felt in those schools where evolution is now being taught as fact.

The Piltdown fraud

There was another piece of evidence supposedly showing human descent from ape-like ancestors which was used at the Tennessee Monkey trial: this was the famous Piltdown Man. Dawn Man, as he was also called, appeared to be a creature that had both ape-like and human-like characteristics and reconstructions of him were on prominent display in natural history museums all over the world. He was proudly displayed in the Tennessee court room as proof that humans had ape-like ancestors. Here was incontrovertible proof that humans had descended from apes and it was also proof that the first ape-people were British! But what was not known at the time was that Piltdown Man was a fraud. The perpetrator (or perpetrators) of this hoax has never been positively identified, and as all the people associated with the finds of Piltdown Man are now dead, it is unlikely that we shall ever really know who was responsible for this deception.

The story of Piltdown Man goes something like this. According to Charles Dawson, a local archaeologist, some labourers were digging in a gravel pit near Piltdown in Sussex at the beginning of the century when they found a few pieces of old bones. Realizing their potential value, their employer gave them to Dawson, and he verified their antiquity and pronounced that they were parts of a skull which was possibly human. Dawson began to search for the rest of the skull and in 1912 a jawbone was uncovered. Arthur Woodward of the British Museum verified that the bones were ancient, and that the skull had human features and that the jaw was ape-like. Whether the jaw fitted the skull could not be determined as the point of attachment or joint on the jaw was missing. The fossils became known as Piltdown Man and were called *Eoanthropus dawsoni* which means 'Dawson's Dawn Man'.

In 1915 another Dawn Man was found in a gravel pit adjacent to the site of the original find. Uncovered in the same stratum were a rhinoceros tooth, a canine tooth and parts of a cranium having human characteristics. This supported the conclusions reached from the first find.

At first, Dawn Man was *the* evolutionary line, but with the discovery of *Homo erectus*, the Neanderthals and the Australopithecines, anthropologists became more and more puzzled in deciding where Piltdown Man fitted into the evolutionary descent of humans. Although it is fairly well known that the names of Dawson and Woodward are associated with the discovery of Piltdown Man, the names of those associated with its being proved to be a fake are not so well known. These are Dr Kenneth Oakley, in collaboration with J. S. Weiner and W. le Gros Clark. In 1953, some forty years after its initial discovery, J. S. Weiner of the University of Oxford began a thorough scientific investigation of Piltdown Man. First of all he examined casts of the fossil and realized that the only true human characteristic of the jaw was the flat wear of the teeth; all other features were ape-like. Unless the teeth had been ground down to make them appear human, modifications of muscle attachments should be present, but they were absent. The canine tooth showed abnormally heavy wear for its age, unless it, too, had been ground down. Furthermore, the biting surfaces did not match. Weiner also discovered that when an orang-utan's tooth was ground down and stained with permanganate, it looked very much like that of the Piltdown Man.

Obviously Weiner had cast doubts on the authenticity of Piltdown Man, so the British Museum authorities were persuaded to allow tests to be carried out on the original finds, rather than on the casts. First of all, X-rays showed that the roots were not human. Then it was shown that the fluorine content of the jaw and teeth was different from the cranium; this meant that the jaw and cranium could not belong to the same individual. Further tests showed that the cranium had been stained with potassium dichromate and the jaw with Van Dyke brown, a colour containing iron. According to Woodward, Dawson had applied the potassium dichromate to harden the fossils, but the question that remained to be answered was why the jaw was stained with Van Dyke brown. Experiments showed that the flints associated with the find had also been iron-stained. Animal teeth found at the site were not only stained, but were also of recent origin and were inconsistent with other animal remains that had been found in the same rock strata.

Piltdown Man was therefore exposed as a forgery. The human skull and orang-utan's jaw had been deliberately fashioned to resemble the infamous missing link. The bones, together with material from other sites, had been deliberately planted in the excavated areas. The nation was so shocked that this forgery had gone undetected for so long that a motion was tabled in the House of Commons 'That the House has no confidence in the Trustees of the British Museum.'

Who was responsible for this ingenious forgery? Many people have accused Dawson because missing links were his special concern. He had an inventory of many fossils and was known to have experimented with staining. Although he had gained a reputation for scrupulous investigation, it was discovered that his finds were not documented. However, no one has ever established a satisfactory motive for Dawson to do such a thing. Malcolm Bowden, on the other hand, has made an excellent case for Teilard de Chardin being the perpetrator of the Piltdown hoax.[4] He was the actual discoverer of several of the fake items and he had access, from a previous assignment in Egypt, to mammalian bones that formed part of the 'imported' fauna at Piltdown. He also had sufficient knowledge to know which animal fossils should be implanted in the gravel to authenticate the finds. He had a considerable knowledge of chemistry and had experimented in staining bones.

But if Teilard de Chardin was the culprit, what were his motives for perpetrating such a hoax? Allow Malcolm Bowden to answer this question for us: 'To discover the answer we must consider the situation in the field of anthropology about 1910. Darwin had predicted a link between man and apes in his *Origin of Species* over fifty years before. The only fossils to support this theory were Dubois' hotly-contested discovery some thirty years later of Java Man, which was composed of a giant gibbon's skull-cap and a human leg-bone. Nothing had been found for *twenty years* before the Piltdown "discoveries". This lack of convincing evidence would obviously be exasperating to those who fanatically supported Darwin's theory... I would suggest that this would provide sufficient motivation for one or more persons to give a "nudge" to the evidence which was so reluctantly forthcoming.'[5]

Furthermore, according to Richard Leakey and Roger Lewin, the discovery of Piltdown Man 'fitted very well the notion that human ancestors must have had a large brain and that the "upgrading" of the rest of the body from ape-like to man-like form trailed behind.'[6]

So we can see that Piltdown Man was uncritically accepted as being a genuine ape-person for a number of decades because it fitted the evolutionists' preconceptions.

Footprints in stone

So far we have considered some of the unfortunate mistakes that have been made by the evolutionists and that have resulted in the reconstructions of fanciful scenarios regarding the history of humanity. Unfortunately, such blunders have not been confined solely to the evolutionists, for recently it has been shown that many creationists have been tripped up by some fossilized footprints that have been found in and around the town of Glen Rose in the state of Texas.

Recognizable dinosaur tracks have been found in the Cretaceous limestone in the surrounding areas of Glen Rose for many years. Along with these dinosaur tracks were some footprints which looked decidedly human. In the late 1960s and early 1970s Stan Taylor of Films for Christ made a film about these tracks entitled *Footprints in Stone*. The object of the film was to show that dinosaur tracks and human tracks had been found in the same rock strata and so dinosaurs and people must have lived at the same time. If this was so, then obviously there was something drastically wrong with the evolutionary geological time-table, for this teaches that man and dinosaurs were separated in time by millions of years.

Unfortunately, very little systematic scientific investigation was carried out on these human-like tracks. However, in the late summer of 1970, Dr Berney Neufeld, Dr Leonard Brand and Dr Arthur Chadwick carried out a fairly detailed study of them. They noticed that: 'The tracks had a clear humanoid appearance, but lacked some of the most important characteristics. There were no clear pentamerous feet, and the profile was more elongate and narrow than one would expect for a human track.'[7]

Furthermore, a careful study of the footprints showed that in several cases there were three unmistakable divisions at the anterior end of the prints and this led them to conclude that the footprints were probably made by a sauropod dinosaur walking in water too shallow for normal tracks. They also noticed that: 'Several of the poorly defined depressions exhibited the elongated appearance of the "man tracks", but further along they became clearly defined as dinosaurian.'[8] Although they had some doubt as to what had made the elongated tracks, they were certain that: 'They did not provide irrefutable evidence of the co-existence of man and dinosaur.'[9]

Dr Neufeld carefully sectioned a genuine dinosaur footprint in several places and he observed that the fine laminations which could be seen in the rock bent downwards in conformity to the track - as would be expected if the animal had stepped in soft mud. However, similar cross-sections of so-called human footprints that had been removed from the Paluxy River bed at Glen Rose and which had been housed in Columbia Union College in Takoma Park, Maryland, did not show any evidence of such deformation.

These findings introduced an element of doubt into believing that human tracks had been found at Glen Rose. Although Dr Neufeld published the results of his investigations,[10] they were either ignored or not noticed. I, for one, did not come across this work until June 1988, when I was researching for this particular section of this book.

Glen Kuban, a young computer programmer from Ohio, was also unaware of Neufeld's article when in 1980 he began a series of expeditions to the Glen Rose area in order to document the fossil human-like tracks as evidence for creation. It was not long before he realized that the tracks were not human, and that he needed to document this. For two years he worked alone, but in 1982 he met Ron Hastings, a local high school physics teacher. Hastings was annoyed by the exaggerated claims that creationists were making about the Paluxy River tracks and he was determined to find out exactly what creature had made the footprints in stone. A third person, Dr Carl Baugh, a Baptist minister, also joined them. Dr Baugh had gone to Glen Rose in the early 1980s hoping to establish a museum of creationist evidence at the site of what was considered by many to be the most famous of all creationist evidences - the Paluxy River human tracks.

The three toiled on and eventually their findings were published.[11] However, towards the end of 1985, before the results of their labours were published, members of the Institute for Creation Research and Paul Taylor of Films for Christ went with Glen Kuban to the site of the tracks, and 'There they saw for themselves evidence that Kuban and Hastings had discovered: surrounding and superimposed on some of the "man-tracks" were discoloured haloes having the unmistakable form of tridactyl sauropod [that is, three-toed dinosaur] tracks. While the origin of the discolourations was not clear, the evidence was compelling. The tracks had to be dinosaurian.'[12]

One member of staff from the Institute for Creation Research who was present at the site was Dr John Morris. In 1980, he had written a book about these tracks in which he had concluded that: 'The evidence already available should be sufficient to convince all but the most sceptical. If one allows the whole body of data to speak for itself, without attempting to harmonize it with preconceived ideas, the conclusion that man and dinosaur walked together at the same time and place - and that both perished in a watery cataclysm - seems inevitable.'[13]

On his return to the headquarters of the Institute for Creation Research in San Diego, Dr Morris wrote an ICR Impact article retracting the positions he and the Institute for Creation Research had taken on the character and significance of the tracks.[14] In an open letter to all those who received this ICR Impact article, Dr Henry Morris, President of the Institute for Creation Research, stated: 'Although the evidence is inconclusive, it must be recognized that a number of fossil tracks formerly regarded as probably man-tracks now seem to show features which are best interpreted in terms of some unidentified two-legged reptile or other animal. Further studies are under way, but creationists should not, at least for the present, cite these particular footprints as evidence against evolution.' Furthermore, as a result of visiting Glen Rose with Glen Kuban, Paul Taylor withdrew from circulation the film *Footprints in Stone* that his father Stan Taylor had made at the beginning of the previous decade.

What can we learn from these footprints in stone? First of all it must be emphasized that the creationist position does not depend upon the footprints from the rocks of the Paluxy River being human. It must also be stated clearly that unlike the evolutionists' Piltdown fraud, which was perpetrated with the deliberate intention of deceiving everyone, there was no intended deception on the part of the creationists at Glen Rose; it was a simple misinterpretation of the data. However, creationists must realize that as a result of their ignorance of the earlier findings of Dr Neufeld and his colleagues, the cost to truth was great. In 1987, Professor Chadwick rightly pointed out: 'Creationists might have had the honour of laying aside this misconception ten years ago with little philosophical expense, as a result of their own scientific research. It has now been torn away by individuals, many of whom, unlike Kuban himself, have little regard for the cause of creationism.'[15]

On the one hand, credit must go to the integrity of the staff of the Institute for Creation Research, especially Dr John Morris, for their retraction as soon as they were confronted with the evidence which cast doubt on the footprints being human. Credit must also go to Paul Taylor for so quickly withdrawing the film *Footprints in Stone* from circulation. On the other hand, it is most disappointing to realize that many evolutionists were not prepared to do real scientific research on these footprints but were quick to dismiss the human-like tracks at Glen Rose as nothing but erosion marks, carvings and chisel marks,[16] even though, as we have seen, they were genuine dinosaur tracks!

Another footprint that is often quoted by creationists as disproving evolution is the so-called Meister footprint. On 1 June 1968, William J. Meister found some fossil trilobites embedded in what appeared to be a sandal print in the Cambrian Rocks at Antelope Springs, which is about forty-three miles north-west of Delta in Utah.[17] The footprint measured ten and a half inches in length, three and a half inches wide at the sole and three inches wide at the heel. However, investigations by staff at the Utah Museum of Natural History at the University of Utah have shown that although the trilobites are genuine (*Erathia kingi* species), the supposed sandal print is the result of a natural break which happens to resemble a sandal print.[18]

Genuine fossil human footprints have, however, been found in rocks conventionally dated as being over three and a half million years old. These were found in 1977 by Mary Leakey in Laetoli in East Africa. The human tracks, along with those of many animals (hares, antelopes, gazelles, giraffe, elephant, rhinoceros, pig, hyena and baboon) were found in a cement-like volcanic tuff rock. The people and the animals had walked on recently deposited volcanic ash while it was still wet (presumably as a result of a rainstorm) and as the ash was high in carbonates, it quickly hardened, fossilizing the tracks.

The evidence is that the creature who made these footprints was human because we are told that 'The form of his foot was exactly the same as ours' and that his 'leg structure must have been very similar to our own'.[19] Clearly then we are dealing with human beings. The footprints were, however, made by a man and a woman, and it is possible to guess at their size: 'An anthropological rule of thumb holds that the length of the foot represents about fifteen per cent of an individual's height. On this basis - and it is far from exact - we can estimate the height of the male as perhaps four feet eight inches (1.4 metres); the female would have stood about four feet.'[20]

Interestingly, when these footprints were presented by the mass media, the ape-like nature of the creatures that made them was stressed. For example, the public was told that the footprints were made by small-brained creatures who had just learned to walk upright. However, as short stature and small brain size is no indication of mental ability, the tracks could quite easily have been made by a couple of pygmies.

Where does all this lead us?

If nothing else, I hope that the revelations made in this chapter have made you more cautious in accepting reconstructions of our fossil ancestors as being true reflections of what they actually looked like. We have seen time and again that such reconstructions are no more than the figments of the imagination of the artists who drew them. Such reconstructions also reflect the preconceived ideas of the supposed evolution of people. You may think that such errors as the construction of Nebraska Man from a pig's tooth are uncommon. You may also think that perhaps in the early part of this century the scientists were not as knowledgeable as they are today and so such errors were bound to occur. But even today, such errors continue to be made by those bent on proving that humans had ape-like ancestors.

For example, in 1971 the *National Geographic Magazine* reported the discovery of the Tasaday tribe.[21] Here was a tribe of people living in caves deep in the rain forest on the remote island of Mindanao, 600 miles south-east of Manila in the Philippines. Naked members of this tribe were photographed by the *National Geographic Magazine* using stone tools. Here was a Stone Age tribe living in the Space Age! In 1987, a film crew from Central Television paid a return visit to the Tasaday tribe and the result of this was broadcast the following year.[22] Men and women recognizable from the original media coverage were found living in ordinary huts, raising normal crops, and wearing tatty tee-shirts and frayed jeans. This was not because they had been exposed too often to Western civilization; it was because they had taken part in a hoax! They had never lived in caves, but every time visitors came, they had left their huts, taken off their clothes and played elaborate charades in the caves. Their Stone Age tools turned out to be pebbles that they had picked out of the stream. They had done this for bribes that in fact never materialized. The anthropologists who originally studied these people had seen what their preconceived ideas had wanted them to see.

Even in the 1980s there have been a couple of examples of the evolutionists being deceived by their own preconceived ideas. For example, a skull that was found in Spain and that had been heralded as the oldest example of *Homo* in Eurasia was shown to be the skull of a young donkey. The *Daily Telegraph* ran a story about this on 14 May 1984 with the headline on page 16 running 'Ass is Taken for a Man'. A year earlier, on 28 April 1983, the headline 'Hominid Collarbone Exposed As Dolphin's Rib' ran in the *New Scientist*. The article under this headline reported Dr Tim White of the University of California, Berkeley as putting this mistake 'on a par with two other embarassing *faux pas* by fossil hunters: *Hespero-pithecus,* the fossil pig's tooth that was cited as evidence of very early man in North America, and *Eoanthropus* or "Piltdown Man", the jaw of an orang-utan and the skull of a modern human that were claimed to be the "earliest Englishman",' and it quotes Dr Tim White as saying, 'The problem with a lot of anthropologists is that they want so much to find a hominid that any scrap of bone becomes a hominid bone.'

As we have seen, however, the creationists are not completely blameless when it comes to misinterpreting the fossil evidence, as we saw in the case of the footprints which have been found at Glen Rose, Texas and at Antelope Springs, Utah. Extreme care must be taken by those in both the evolution camp and those in the creation camp so that they do not ignore the facts, nor interpret the data to suit their particular preconceived ideas. One thing is certain, however, and that is that the reconstructions of ape-people as seen in books and in museums are nothing more than figments of the imagination.

5.
With animal connections?

We saw in chapter 3 that the fossils shout a resounding 'No!' to the idea that human beings are the product of evolution. The reason being that the fossil record shows that there are gaps between all the major life-forms. In spite of this, however, these gaps in the fossil record have been used in an attempt to show that instead of evolution proceeding gradually (gradualism), it occurs by a series of 'jumps' (punctuated equilibria). Interestingly, in an article entitled 'Who Doubts Evolution?' Mark Ridley of the Animal Behaviour Research Group at Oxford University has commented on this as follows: 'The argument (i.e. gradualism versus punctuated equilibria) is about the actual historical pattern of evolution; but outsiders, seeing a controversy unfolding, have imagined that it is about the truth of evolution - whether evolution occurred at all. This is a terrible mistake; and it springs, I believe, from the false idea that the fossil record provides an important part of the evidence that evolution took place. In fact, evolution is proven by a totally separate set of arguments - and the present debate within palaeontology does not impinge at all on the evidence that supports evolution.'[1]

According to Mark Ridley then, the fossil record is irrelevant to what he calls 'the truth of evolution'. However, evolutionists have not always argued this way, for as recently as 1979, David Attenborough wrote, 'It [the theory of natural selection] remains the key to our understanding of the natural world and it enables us to recognize that life has a long and continuous history during which organisms, both plant and animal, have changed, generation by generation, as they colonized all parts of the world. The direct, if fragmentary, evidence for this history [of the evolution of life] lies in the archives of the earth, the sedimentary rocks.'[2]

What has happened then to make evolutionists change their minds about the fossil record? As pointed out in an earlier chapter, since the early 1970s two American palaeontologists, Dr Niles Eldredge and Professor Stephen Jay Gould, have pointed out that palaeontologists cannot show the gradual evolution of one life-form into another in the fossil record - there are real gaps, as we have seen. This fact has been taken up by the creationists much to the annoyance of evolutionists. So now that it is recognized that the fossil record contains these gaps, the palaeontologists tell us that it cannot be used to show that evolution has not occurred. For example, Professor Michael Ruse has written, 'The creationists spend a great deal of time on the fossil record. This in itself is a misleading tactic, for the fossil record has always been but one part of the evolutionary spectrum. Picking out the record for such extended discussion gives a false picture of evolutionary studies. In fact, evolutionists turn for insight and support to all areas of biology: biogeography, morphology, embryology, systematics and so forth. And yet, creationists hurry through these fields, barely mentioning them, if at all.'[3]

So that such an accusation cannot be made of me, it is my intention to spend time in this chapter looking at some other scientific disciplines, to see if they present proof that people are connected to the animals and are the product of evolution. The first area I want us to consider is one that is mentioned specifically by Professor Ruse - that of embryology. What support, if any, does this give to the idea that humans are evolved apes?

Embryonic recapitulation

Put simply, embryonic recapitulation means that as the embryo develops, it goes through phases wherein stages of its supposed evolution are recaptured. This 'theory' was proposed and greatly popularized by the German scientist Professor Ernst Haeckel who lived from 1834-1917. Professor Haeckel called embryonic recapitulation a 'great biogenetic law' and maintained that it seemed to him to prove evolution without a shadow of a doubt, for by watching an embryo develop he maintained that you could see it pass through its various ancestral life-forms. He argued that by watching the human embryo develop you could see it develop from a single cell to a worm-stage, then a fish-stage (characterized by gill-slits), then an amphibian-stage, then a mammalian-stage (complete with tail), before it finally developed into a human being.

Probably the most well-known and oft-quoted evidence in support of embryonic recapitulation is the so-called fish-stage of our embryonic development. As the human embryo develops, a stage is reached when it has folds of skin, which resemble gill slits on each side of its body. But they are not gills at all, and they cannot be used for breathing, which is the function of gills. They are formed because the unequal rate of growth of the central nervous system and the arterial systems causes the month-old embryo to bow itself over the heart bulge. The resulting folds develop into arches which in turn develop into the lower jaw, the tongue and other organs such as the eustachian tubes that connect the throat and the middle ear. Hence to argue that the human embryo goes through a fish-stage and has gill-slits shows a complete lack of understanding of embryonic development.

The various stages through which an embryo passes as it develops from a single cell to a complex organism are necessary. Organs and structures in the human embryo that look similar to those in animals do not, in many cases, ever have the function of that organ or structure. For example, as we have seen, the so-called 'gill-slits' in the human embryo never have a respiratory function. Furthermore, many of the stages that you would expect to find are absent, and others, such as the early stages of the human heart, occur in the 'wrong' order. As the heart develops in the human embryo, it does have one chamber (as in a worm), then two chambers (as in the fish), then three chambers (as in the frog) and then four chambers with a connection of the two sides (as in a reptile). But the embryo starts out with a two-chambered heart and the two chambers then fuse into one for a time, before developing into two, three and finally four chambers. Thus the early stages occur in the 'wrong' evolutionary order.

Other developments within the embryo confirm designed co-ordinated development. One such development is the way in which the diaphragm (the muscle we use in order to breathe) and the phrenic nerve (the nerve that connects our diaphragm to the spinal cord) are formed. The way the diaphragm and the phrenic nerve

develop in the embryo does not mimic any supposed evolutionary
transition from fish to man, but shows a designed, co-ordinated
development, displaying plan and purpose right from the start: 'An
embryo starts off as a flat plate of tissue consisting of three layers.
This must be folded up so that the top layer ends up being the
outside layer. The piece of tissue destined to become the major part
of the diaphragm actually starts off "above" the part which will
become the head. When the embryo folds up, this piece of tissue,
called the *septum transversum,* is swung around to end up in front
of the neck. Here, muscle-forming cells move into it. Evolution
cannot make the slightest sense of this. This developing muscle
tissue is already connected to the third, fourth and fifth spinal cord
segments. The *septum transversum* now moves down the body to
make way for the heart which grows downwards from a little tube
in the neck region. Thus, muscle tissue from the neck is carried
down the body by the developing diaphragm, dragging its nerve
supply behind it.'[4]

If embryonic recapitulation does not occur, then why was Professor Haeckel so adamant that it does? Why did it seem to him to
prove evolution without a shadow of a doubt? Malcolm Bowden
and Francis Hitching have done some remarkable homework about
Professor Haeckel,[5] and I am indebted to them for some of the
following revelations about the professor and his 'biogenetic law'.

First of all, let us consider why Professor Haeckel could write
the following: 'When we see that at a certain stage the embryos of
man and the ape, the dog and the rabbit, the pig and the sheep,
though recognizable as vertebrates, cannot be distinguished from
each other, the fact can only be elucidated by assuming a common
parentage...I have illustrated this significant fact by a juxtaposition
of corresponding stages in the development of different vertebrates
in my *Natural History of Creation* and in my *Anthropogeny*.'[6] The
reason is quite simple: Professor Haeckel doctored his drawings of
embryos to make them look the same! The embryos of humans,
apes, dogs, rabbits, pigs and sheep do *not* look the same, but they
do in Professor Haeckel's drawings, because he chopped off bits
here and there, and added on bits elsewhere so that they seemed
identical.

Such forgeries and falsifications are well-documented.[7] For
example, in order to illustrate the worm-like stage of embryonic
development, Professor Haeckel published three *identical* draw-

ings, which he labelled a dog, a chicken and a turtle, respectively. The drawings were identical, for he had used the *same* woodcut (of the embryo of a dog) three times. This forgery was exposed in 1868 by L. Rutimeyer, Professor of Zoology and Comparative Anatomy at the University of Basel in Switzerland.[8] According to Francis Hitching, over the years, various other forgeries were exposed: 'To illustrate the "embryo of a Gibbon in the fish-stage", Haeckel used the embryo of a different kind of monkey altogether, and then sliced off those parts of the anatomy inconvenient to his theory, such as arms, legs, heart, navel and other non-fishy appendages. Another time, he altered the shape of embryological drawings to make the braincases of fishes, frogs, tortoises and chickens look the same.'[9]

Since as an embryo develops, it does *not* in fact recapture its supposed evolutionary ancestry, why is it that this idea has gained so much support? The answer is that Professor Haeckel was extremely successful in popularizing this idea. However, Professor Haeckel was not an honest man and he faked his embryonic drawings in order for them to support his 'biogenetic law'. Not only did Professor Haeckel doctor and falsify his drawings, but he also invented some! He inserted imaginary animals so that he could produce a neatly graduated progression showing the evolution of simple to complex. It must not be forgotten that his readers were given no indication that some of the animals were real and some the product of his imagination. Furthermore, on one occasion he extended the thirty-three vertebrae of a human to thirty-five and then added a tail (containing a further nine) giving a total of forty-four in all.[10] Professor Haeckel also drew the head of an ape on the body of a man - the elusive missing link!

His forgeries were well known, and he was eventually charged with fraud by five professors at a university court at Jena.   Although he admitted that he had altered his drawings, surprisingly, he was never publicly disgraced nor even dimissed from his post. Professor Haeckel was unrepentant. One writer has reported him as saying, 'A small per cent of my embryonic drawings are forgeries; those, namely, for which the observed material is so incomplete or insufficient as to compel us to fill in and reconstruct the missing links by hypothesis and comparative synthesis. I should feel utterly condemned and annihilated by the admission, were it not that hundreds of the best observers and biologists lie under the same charge. The great majority of all morphological, anatomical, histological, and embryological diagrams are not true to nature but are more or less doctored, schematized, and reconstructed.'[11]

And in 1908, Haeckel wrote the following to a Berlin newspaper in defence of his forgeries: 'To cut short this unsavoury dispute, I begin at once with the contrite confession that a small fraction of my numerous drawings of embryos (perhaps six or eight per cent) are in a sense falsified - all those, namely, for which the present material of observation is so incomplete or insufficient as to compel us, when we come to prepare a continuous chain of evolutionary stages, to fill up the gaps by hypotheses, and to reconstruct the missing links by comparative synthesis... After this compromising confession of "forgery" I should be obliged to consider myself "condemned and annihilated" if I had not the consolation of seeing side by side with me in the prisoner's dock hundreds of fellow-culprits, among many of the most trusted observers and most esteemed biologists. The great majority of all of the diagrams in the best biological textbooks, treatises and journals would incur in the same degree the charge of "forgery", for all of them are inexact, and are more or less doctored, schematized and constructed.'[12] In other words, he used the excuse that everyone else was forging their drawings, so why shouldn't he do the same?

Embryonic recapitulation does not therefore rest on fact but on falsified as well as fictitious drawings. Today it is generally discounted although occasionally a modern textbook on biology will still publish some of Haeckel's drawings in support of this idea. One thing, however, is certain and that is that human development does not pass through developmental stages of fish, turtle or dog; it is specifically human right from the beginning.[13]

Vestigial organs

The existence of vestigial organs in the human body is often cited as evidence for its evolution. Vestigial organs are organs or structures that are considered to have no use or purpose in their present form, but to have had a use in previous forms and therefore to represent a sort of vestige of that organ. They are seen to be in the process of evolutionary decay and can therefore be expected to disappear completely during the course of future evolution.

The crucial question is: 'Does the human body have any vestigial organs, that is, organs that no longer serve any useful purpose in our bodies?' Much of the identification of vestigial organs, especially in the human body, was done by the German anatomist Wiedersheim. In his book *The Structure of Man*,[14] Wiedersheim gave a list of eighty-six vestigial organs as well as many others he considered to be retrogressive. Some of the organs listed as vestigial and having no function at all included the pineal body, the pituitary gland and the lachrymal glands. Wiedersheim's list has been investigated thoroughly by S. R. Scadding of the Department of Zoology at the University of Guelph, Ontario, Canada and he has concluded: 'On the basis of this analysis, I would suggest that Wiedersheim was largely in error in compiling his long list of vestigial organs. Most of them do have at least a minor function at some point in life.'[15]

In other words, as our knowledge of physiology has increased, it has been found that these organs do have some purpose. In fact, in one biology textbook, it has been suggested 'that the term "vestigial" is really a word biologists use in place of admitting their ignorance of the function of some organ'.[16]

Yet in spite of the fact that our bodies do not contain function-less vestigial organs, examples of vestigial organs in the human body are still cited in modern biology textbooks. The most common examples given are the appendix, the coccyx (often referred to as the vestige of the human tail) and the semilunar fold of the eye (often called the third eyelid). But all of these organs perform a function and should not therefore be considered as vestigial. In fact, Scadding points out: 'Anatomically, the appendix shows evidence of a lymphoid function since the submucosa is much thickened and almost entirely occupied by lymphatic nodules and lymphocytes. There is experimental evidence as well that the veriform appendix is a lymphoid organ which acts as a reservoir of antibody producing cells. The coccyx serves as a point of insertion for several muscles and ligaments including the *gluteus maximus*. The semilunar fold of the eye is simply that portion of the conjunctiva at the medial corner of the eye and as such aids in the cleansing and lubrication of the eyeball. Similarly, for other "vestigial organs" there are reasonable grounds for supposing that they are functional albeit in a minor way.'[17]

Hence to say that such organs as the appendix, coccyx and the semilunar fold of the eye are vestigial because they serve no useful function is to exhibit a complete lack of understanding of the functions of these organs. The human body does not contain any vestigial organs and so such a concept cannot be used to support the idea that humans have evolved from other creatures.

Another category of so-called vestigial organs are those which are the remnants of the reproductive structures of the opposite sex. The most obvious and widely cited example is the nipples on men. Such structures, however, reflect the embryonic development of the human foetus which begins its physical development in what may be called a sexually indifferent condition with structures characteristic of both sexes. These structures are not evidence of our evolutionary development, because no one supposes that males evolved from females or vice versa. Thus the similarities that exist between men and women are nothing at all to do with evolution, but are clearly due to a similar design by a Creator.

Comparative anatomy

Comparative anatomy is the science that deals with the structure of animals and although it is often considered to be strong evidence for evolution, in fact it can be used as evidence of creation, as we shall see.

The bones of a horse are different from our bones, but there is such a similarity that if we are familiar with the human skeleton, we could easily identify and name the bones of a horse. Similarly, we could do the same thing when studying the skeleton of a salamander, a crocodile, a bird and a bat. Not only are the bones similar, but also other structures such as muscles, heart, liver, kidneys, eyes, digestive tracts and so on. This is interpreted as being proof that all these various animals are descended from one common ancestor.

One of the classic examples that is often used in biology textbooks to illustrate comparative anatomy is the forelimbs of amphibians, reptiles, humans, birds, bats and quadrupeds. In the illustration,[18] it can be seen that all the forelimbs of these six different types of creatures have an upper arm bone (the humerus) and two lower arm bones (the radius and the ulna), although in the case of the bat, these two bones are fused into one bone called the radio-ulna. These structures are said to be homologous when they are similar in structure and origin, but not necessarily in function. Notice how subtly the notion of origins is introduced into the definition. The bat's wing is therefore considered to be homologous to the forelimb of a salamander, but not to the wing of an insect (which has the same function). However, the fact that the two structures are similar does not necessarily mean that they are derived from a common ancestor.

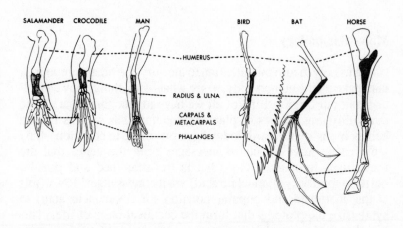

We must realize that the entire line of reasoning by evolutionists is based upon one single assumption: that the degree of similarity of organisms indicates the degree of supposed relationship of the said organisms. In other words, it is argued that if animals look alike, then they must be related; if they do not look very much alike, then they are more distantly related. But this is just an assumption, and none of the 'evidences' from similarity can be used to demonstrate genetic relationships among organisms. This should be required if real empirical evidence for evolution (that is, the change of one kind of animal into another) is to be obtained. Therefore animals that are similar are not necessarily related.

How then can comparative anatomy be used as evidence for creation? When God created the vertebrates, for example, he used a single blueprint for the body plan, but varied the plan so that each different kind of vertebrate would be perfectly equipped to take its place in the wonderful world that he had created. Hence the variation in the bone structure of the forelimbs of the different kinds of vertebrates that we have considered. If all vertebrates had a common ancestor, as the evolutionist so emphatically claims, then there should be a continuous intergradation between all the various kinds of vertebrates. Instead, there are great gaps between the different kinds, both in the present world and in the fossil record. This is not only true for the vertebrates, but also for all other animals, as well as plants. Only creation with variation within limits can account for *both* similarities and differences.

Molecular biology

I want us now to turn our attention to the very chemical compounds that make up the human body, to see what, if anything, they can tell us about our origins. First of all we have to recognize that all the many different species of plants and animals, as well as human beings living on the earth today have one thing in common - they are all kept alive by coded messages from the genes that are transmitted from the DNA (that is the shortened and popular notation for deoxyribonucleic acid) via its 'messenger' RNA (this is the shortened and popular notation for ribonucleic acid) to synthesize the proteins that form the chemical basis of life. This bio-chemical universal (the term which is given to properties shared by all living things) is not unique: 'All proteins are made up of the same twenty amino acids, in differing proportions. All life is structured from cells of about the same size, which divide and renew themselves in a remarkably similar way. The spiral structure of DNA, with its links consisting of just four nucleotide acids, is also common to everything alive.'[19]

According to the evolutionist, these biochemical universals, especially the universality of the genetic code, prove that all the living creatures on earth have evolved from a common ancestor - the first self-replicating system which contained DNA, together with the genetic code. This is supposed to have come into existence purely as a result of chance natural forces.

Reading popular articles on the origin of life and listening to the pronouncements of the media, we are given the impression that there is overwhelming proof that living systems have evolved from non-living inorganic compounds. The results of the now famous Miller experiment[20] in which a mixture of methane, ammonia, hydrogen and water vapour produced simple amino acids under conditions which were supposed to have been in existence on the pre-biotic earth, are often cited as proof that life arose from non-life. But there are major problems with such a line of reasoning.

First of all it is believed that the atmosphere of the early earth was composed of a mixture of gases similar to that used in Miller's experiment and that it contained no oxygen. But if it contained no oxygen, then there would have been no ozone layer around the earth. Hence the surface of the earth would have been bombarded with ultra-violet radiation and this would have destroyed any amino acids that had been formed. Had oxygen been present in the atmosphere, then the amino acids would not have been synthesized from such a mixture of gases in the first place. So the problem is this: without oxygen, amino acids would not have survived; with oxygen, amino acids would not have formed.

Another problem is that so far it has proved impossible to synthesize five of the twenty amino acids which are common to living creatures in conditions which, according to the evolutionist, are likely to have occurred on the pre-biotic earth. In order to 'solve' this problem, some chemical evolutionists propose either that some of the essential organic chemicals occurred naturally on the pre-biotic earth [21](how this 'natural' occurrence came about is not explained) while others propose that they came to earth on meteorites or comets,[22] (how they got there in the first place is not explained, so the problem is just pushed one step further back in space and time).

A further problem is that the synthesis of proteins is a puzzle. We are all familiar with the conundrum: which came first, the chicken or the egg? There is a similar, and one could say more fundamental conundrum confronting the evolutionist: which came first, proteins or DNA? Proteins can be thought of as blocks or strings of amino acids and they react with other chemicals to form nucleic acids, including DNA. Proteins, however, are produced by DNA. Hence DNA is dependent upon proteins for its formation and, in turn, proteins are dependent upon DNA for their formation. One evolutionist has posed this conundrum in the form of the question: 'How, when no life existed, did substances come into being which, today, are absolutely essential to living systems, yet which can only be formed by those systems?'[23] No one knows the answer to this question according to a recent pronouncement by another evolutionist.[24] The famous chemical evolutionist Professor Sidney Fox of the University of Miami has answered the question by saying simply, 'Whichever postulate has been considered has seemed to leave an unresolved question.'[25]

There is yet another problem with the origin of DNA and that is that the evolution of DNA with its genetic code is a complete mystery. The September 1978 edition of *Scientific American* was devoted solely to the subject of evolution. In an article about the evolution of life in this journal, Professor Richard Dickerson wrote, 'The evolution of the genetic machinery is the step for which there are no laboratory models; hence one can speculate endlessly, unfettered by inconvenient facts.'[26]

And more recently, the famous chemical evolutionist Professor Leslie Orgel has stated: 'We must next explain how a pre-biotic soup of organic molecules, including amino acids and the organic constituents of nucleotides, evolved into a self-replicating organism. While some suggestive evidence has been obtained, I must admit that attempts to reconstruct this evolutionary process are extremely tentative.'[27]

So the explanations for the evolution of the genetic code, however good and emphatic they may sound, are no more than tentative speculations! Such speculations have been reviewed by the creationist biochemist Dr Duane Gish,[28] and I would advise those wishing to pursue this subject further to read Dr Gish's excellent monograph.

There are also some other puzzles about DNA, as pointed out by Francis Hitching.[29] One is that there is no one-for-one correlation between genes and outward appearance - you can get more than one protein from the same DNA sequence. Another is that the DNA in chimpanzees differs from our own by less than one per cent; yet geneticists expect a far bigger difference to account for the enormous dissimilarity between the two creatures. A further puzzle is that that there appears to be no obvious advantage in having large quantities of DNA. For example, although humans have about a hundred times as much DNA as bacteria, a salamander has twenty times as much as a human being.

It is not only because of these real scientific problems about the origin and evolution of DNA that creationists believe in creation, but it is also because they find it rational to believe in the Creator being the author of life. The chemical instructions for the construction of a complete human being exist in every fertilized human egg. Dr John Gribbin has shown that one chromosome may contain the information equivalent to 500,000,000 words.[30] With about 400 words on a page, one chromosome therefore contains information equivalent to 5,435 books each 230 pages long. As humans have forty-six chromosomes, you would therefore need a library of a quarter of a million of such books to store all the information contained in every fertilized human egg. To the evolutionist, this is no proof that the 'writing' found on the genes in the fertilized egg has been either written or developed by a Creator. For the evolutionist, the laws of nature and the properties of matter have written and designed everything. Furthermore, to the evolutionist, the universality of the genetic code is proof of evolution - that every organism has a common ancestor, which was the first living cell to have this genetic code.

This genetic code supposedly arose by chance. We are told that the nucleotides, deoxyribose and the guanine, thymine, uracil, cytosine and adenine molecules formed the DNA molecule (in helical form) under the influence of the laws of nature which are present in all matter. At the same time (or with time) the grammar, punctuation and correction mechanisms (necessary, should faults develop) of the genetic language developed under the same influence of the same laws of nature. Evolutionists inform us that chance and the laws of nature then provided the chemical instructions to make eyes, ears, hearts, kidneys, livers, brains, hair, bone, teeth, muscles and so on - indeed all the parts to make a complete human being.

If the evolutionist is correct in his belief that living systems are the product of chance and the laws of nature, then the laws of thermodynamics must be in error for these laws show that matter does not have project-content nor teleology (that is, interpretation in terms of purpose). For example, if matter is agitated, it will *not* build a machine. Chance will *not* plan and make a machine, nor will it produce an understandable language that will in turn build biological machines such as human beings.

As Professor Wilder-Smith points out in his book *He Who Thinks Has To Believe*,[31] in reality the evolutionist is asking us to believe that the paper on which the text of a book is written has developed not only the language in which the book is written, but also all its concepts, ideas and thoughts - in other words, that the paper wrote the entire book! Creationists, on the other hand, believe in an Author who wrote the book of life - just as any other book, without exception, was written by an author and not by the paper. Life consists of various genetic books - a different genetic book for each kind of life. But as the genetic language (that is the genetic code) is identical in all forms of life (only the content varies, according to the kind of life) the creationists believe in a single personal Author, who always employs the same language to store and realize all his ideas, projects and life concepts. Hence the universality of the genetic code. Therefore, far from proving evolution, the universality of the genetic code is consistent with the idea of a Creator.

Before we leave DNA, I want to comment briefly on the recent pronouncement by a group of scientists working at the University of California, Berkeley that they have traced back the family tree of the whole human race to one original woman who lived in Africa.[32] This has been done by studying the structure of the mitochondrial DNA which is passed down from one generation to the next through the female line. As a result of this pronouncement, a number of articles have appeared in the popular scientific press and the BBC devoted a complete *Horizon* programme to it in 1987. More often than not, the popular interpretation given to these findings is that Eve has been identified.

However, we must be careful not to jump to conclusions too hastily. As pointed out by Dr Nancy Darrall, although the scientific findings do not contradict the Genesis account, only one of a number of interpretations of the findings is that there was one original woman.[33] Furthermore, an African origin for humans has not been proved by the findings from mitochondrial DNA, for it is based upon an interpretation of the variation found in the mitochondrial DNA of people found in that region. It is really too early to draw any definite conclusions from this line of research at this present time. As Dr Nancy Darrall says, 'We await further developments in this field with interest.'[34]

The last topic in the molecular biological field I want us to look at is cytochrome *c* and evolution. It is taught that the differences in the amino acid sequences in the cytochromes of different animals have proved the evolutionary origin of species. It is true that the cytochromes of different animals are different from each other. For example, the mammals differ among themselves by roughly five amino acids out of 104; mammals differ from birds and reptiles by roughly ten to fifteen residues; fish differ from all the land vertebrates by eighteen to twenty; and insects differ from vertebrates by an average of twenty-six residues. But does this prove evolution?

Let us look at the way in which the evolutionist argues that such differences prove that evolution has occurred. It is argued that if you compare these differences in the amino acid sequences in the cytochrome c of any two species, the further apart the species are on the evolutionary tree, the more unlike their cytochromes are. It is argued that you can then use the differences in the sequences to construct a phylogenetic tree. As this tree is basically the same as the evolutionary tree, it is argued that this is proof of evolution. But is it?

The important thing to notice is that the phylogenetic tree is constructed on the assumption that the further apart the species are on the evolutionary tree, then the more unlike their cytochromes are. In other words, the evolutionary tree has been used to construct an evolutionary tree! This is tautology and so nothing has been proven.

The other thing to notice is that even though there is tautology in that one tree is used to construct the other, there are quite a number of important disagreements between them. Some of these have been enumerated by Professor Francisco Ayala of the University of California at Davis, when he wrote, 'The cytochrome c phylogeny disagrees with the traditional one in several instances, including the following: the chicken appears to be related more closely to the penguin than to ducks and pigeons; the turtle, a reptile, appears to be related more closely to birds than to the rattlesnake, and man and monkey diverge from mammals before the marsupial kangaroo separates from the placental mammals.'[35]

So, far from proving the accepted evolutionary account of the origin of species, the account according to the cytochrome c phylogenetic tree actually disagrees with it in many details.

From the point of view of the creationist, again you would expect there to be differences in the amino acid sequences of cytochromes of different animals. The Creator used a blueprint and varied it according to the kind of creature he was making. The differences in the amino acid sequences in the cytochromes of different animals are therefore an indication of creation, not evolution.

Races

Before we leave the subject of molecular biology with its DNA molecule and the genetic code, I want us to look at one other related subject - that of race. The existence of the many different races of people on the earth is not thought of as a problem for the evolutionist, rather it is considered to be a problem for the creationist. Is it possible for two people (Adam and Eve) to give rise to all the different types of people that we have on the earth today? Human beings come in all different shades and sizes: from being very dark, like those from Central Africa, to very fair, like those from Scandinavian countries; from being very short, like the pygmies, to being very tall, like the Zulus, and so on. This tremendous amount of variation within the humankind is often considered a challenge to creationists' belief that 'From one man he [God] made every nation of men, that they should inhabit the whole earth; and he determined the times set for them and the exact places where they should live.'[36]

Two different genealogical trees of humankind have been published by Dr Colin Patterson, a zoologist who works at the British Museum (Natural History).[37] Tree A is based on anthropologists' measurements and comparisons of twenty-six external features, such as eye, hair and skin colour, limb proportions and facial characteristics, whereas tree B is based on differences in fifty-eight genetic markers, mostly blood proteins. As pointed out by Dr Colin Patterson, a cynic might suppose that tree A was produced by racist anthropologists and that tree B gives the true history of human differentiation. However, he does not think this is so; he believes that although tree B is nearer the truth, it is likely that the two trees differ mainly because the external features used in tree A are adaptations to climate, so that the tree recognizes climatic groups.

But is it possible for these nine different types of people to have been produced from a single pair and in a relatively short period of time? This question has been answered in the affirmative by Dr Gary Parker in an article which refers to the work of Francisco Ayala, Professor of Genetics at the University of California at Davis and Director of the Institute of Ecology there.[38] Professor

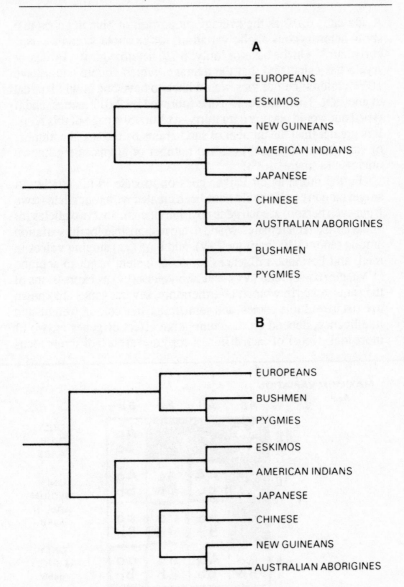

Two different genealogical trees of human populations

Ayala cites 6.7% as the average proportion of human genes that show heterozygous allelic variation, for example straight versus curly hair.[39] On the basis of 'only' 6.7% heterozygosity, Professor Ayala has calculated that the average human couple could have 10^{2017} children before they would have to have one child identical to another! This number is a one followed by 2,017 zeroes, and if typed out would occupy over thirty-six lines of a page of this book. It is greater than the number of sand grains by the sea, the number of stars in the sky, and even the number of atoms in the known universe (a 'mere' 10^{80})!

Furthermore, as Dr Parker goes on to state in his article: 'A single human couple could have been created with four alleles (two from each person) at each gene position (locus). Just two alleles for vocal cord characteristics, V and v, are responsible for the variation among tenor (VV), baritone (Vv), and bass (vv) singing voices in men, and hormone influences on development result in soprano (VV), mezzo-soprano (Vv), and alto voices (vv) as expressions of the same genes in women. Furthermore, several genes are known to exist in multiple copies, and some traits, like colour, weight, and intelligence, depend on the cumulative effect of genes at two or more loci. Genes of each different copy and at each different locus

MAXIMUM VARIATION
AaBb x AaBb

	AB	*Ab*	*aB*	*ab*	
AB	AA BB			Aa Bb	ONLY DARK AABB
Ab		AA bb	Aa Bb	Aa bb	ONLY MEDIUM AAbb or aaBB
aB		Aa Bb	aa BB	aa Bb	
ab	Aa Bb	Aa bb	aa Bb	aa bb	ONLY LIGHT aabb

Genetic square for human skin colour variation

could exist in four allelic forms, so the potential for diversity is staggering indeed!'[40]

But what about the time factor? How long would it take, for example, to produce all the different shades of human skin colour we have today? Dr Parker points out that 'There are several factors that contribute subtle tones to skin colours, but all people have *the same* basic skin colouring agent, the protein called *melanin.*'[41] Then, referring to Davenport's study in the West Indies which showed the amount of skin colour we have is influenced by at least two pairs of genes, A-a and B-b, Dr Parker shows that it would only take *one generation* for AaBb parents to have children with all the variations in skin colour that we see today - as demonstrated in the genetic square on the opposite page.

What happened then as the descendants of our first parents (and of Noah's family) multiplied and moved over the earth? Allow me to let Dr Parker answer this question: 'If those with very dark skin colour (AABB) moved into the same area and/or chose to marry only those with very dark skin colour, then all their children would be limited to very dark skin colour. Similarly, children of parents with very light skin colour (aabb) could have only very light skin, since their parents would have only "small a's and b's" to pass on. Parents with genotypes AAbb or aaBB would be limited to producing only children with medium skin colour. But where people of different backgrounds get back together again, as they do in the West Indies, then their children can once again express the full range of variations. Except for mutational loss of skin colour (albinism), then, the human gene pool would be the same now as it might have been at creation - just four genes A,a,B,b, no more and no less.'[42]

However, there are probably more gene loci and more alleles involved and these would make it even easier to store genetic variability in our created ancestors. We can therefore conclude by saying that as our ancestors spread over the earth after the Tower of Babel incident, the variation 'hidden' in the genes of two average-looking parents came to visible expression in different tribes and tongues and nations.

Conclusion

At the beginning of this chapter, we saw that some evolutionists accuse creationists of concentrating their arguments on the fossil record when dealing with the creation/evolution debate. We therefore turned our attention to other areas to see what light, if any, they could shed upon this controversy.

First of all we saw that the idea of embryonic recapitulation does not rest on fact, but is based on falsified as well as fictitious drawings. We then saw that there is no evidence that the human body contains any vestigial organs. The term is a misnomer and has been used to cover up the biologists' ignorance of the functions of various organs in the body. When we turned our attention to comparative anatomy, we saw that the evidence indicates design, as does the findings of molecular biology. Finally, we saw that there are no real scientific problems in believing that all the different races are descended from one human pair in a short period of time.

So far from supporting the idea of evolution, we find that other scientific disciplines actually support the idea of creation. Indeed, there is no evidence that we are related to the animals. The evidence points to the fact that God used a blue-print for his creation of animals and people, and then varied it according to what particular creature he was making. It is comforting to realize that the latest research and recent scientific discoveries make it increasingly possible for us to praise the Lord God with King David, by saying,

'For you created my inmost being;
    you knit me together in my mother's womb.
I praise you because I am fearfully and wonderfully
    made'

(Psalm 139:13-14).

6.
Who was Adam?

This book deals with the ultimate question about our own origins and is really asking the question: 'Are humans evolved apes or were they created human?' In chapters 3 and 4 we spent all our time considering the first part of the question: 'Are we evolved apes?' By examining the fossil record, we saw quite clearly that there is no justification for believing that humans are evolved apes. Not only is there no evidence that humans have evolved from ape-like ancestors, but there is no evidence for the evolution of one life-form into another. We saw that artistic impressions of our supposed ape-like ancestors are nothing but the figments of the artists' imagination and that ape-men and ape-women have only ever existed in drawings found in both popular books as well as text-books on evolution. Indeed, we saw that in one very important case, the ape-man called Nebraska Man was constructed from the tooth of an extinct kind of pig, and in another case the ape-man called Piltdown Man was nothing but a downright fraud. We also considered the evidence that dinosaur footprints and human footprints have been found in the same rock strata, and we saw that we need to be very cautious in uncritically accepting the evidence that is sometimes proffered. We did see, however, that the fossils do shout a resounding 'No!' to evolution.

It was only in the last chapter that we began to consider the second part of the question: 'Were we created human?' We did this by looking at what other scientific evidence is used in an attempt to support the idea of evolution. In each case we saw that the *facts* can be interpreted in terms of creation. So far, however, we have not turned our attention to look at what is recorded in the Bible about human origins. This we will now rectify by considering what the Bible teaches about Adam.

Adam in the Old Testament

In the very first chapter of the Bible, we read the account of the creation. Here, in the beginning, we are confronted not with man, but with God - the Lord God Almighty, the Creator of all things. Here, in this mighty opening chapter of the book of Genesis, we read that God created 'the heaven and earth, the sea, and all that in them is' in six days.[1] And it was not until the sixth day that we read, 'Then God said, "Let us make man in our image, in our likeness, and let them rule over the fish of the sea and the birds of the air, over the livestock, over all the earth, and over all the creatures that move along the ground."

> 'So God created man
>   in his own image,
>   in the image of God
>   he created him;
>   male and female
>   he created them'

(Genesis 1:26-27).

A detailed description of God's creating the first human pair is found in Genesis chapter 2. Some people claim that there is a contradiction between the account of the creation given in Genesis chapter 1 and that given in chapter 2 - but there is not, for the account given in the second chapter complements that given in the first. The significant verses in Genesis chapter 2 about the creation of the first human pair are: 'And the Lord God formed man from the dust of the ground and breathed into his nostrils the breath of life, and the man became a living being... So the Lord God caused the man to fall into a deep sleep; and while he was sleeping, he took one of man's ribs (or part of man's side [footnote]) and closed up the place with flesh. Then the Lord God made a woman from the rib [or part (footnote)] he had taken out of the man, and he brought her to the man' (Genesis 2:7, 21-22).

This is the account of the creation of the first human pair - Adam and his wife Eve. It must be stressed that there is nothing evolutionary in this scriptural account: the first human beings were created by God - they did not evolve from some animal ape-like ancestor.

There are some Christians, however, who maintain that the 'dust of the ground' in Genesis 2:7 is a reference to humankind's evolutionary descent (or ascent, depending on your view of it) via the various life-forms from the first self-replicating molecule that supposedly evolved on the shores of the earth's hypothetical primeval ocean. Such an argument is, however, negated by the Scriptures, for in Genesis 3:19 it is recorded that God said to Adam:

> 'By the sweat of your brow
> you will eat your food
> until you return to the ground,
> since from it you were taken;
> for dust you are
> and to dust you will return.'

The dust (of the ground) that God referred to here is literal dust - the same dust that is referred to in Genesis 2:7, otherwise the argument used by God would not make sense. It would be nonsense to give 'dust of the ground' an evolutionary meaning in Genesis 2:7 and a literal meaning in Genesis 3:19, especially when in Genesis 3:19 there is a clear-cut reference to the fact that Adam was made from the dust of the ground - an obvious reference to Genesis 2:7.

It is therefore obvious that the early chapters of Genesis teach a creation of a real historical pair of humans - Adam and Eve. Yet it is often taught that Adam and Eve were mythical - in other words, that they were not real historical people at all. This, however, is not borne out by the evidence of Scripture for the early chapters of Genesis are written in the language of a narrative. They are not written as poetry nor indeed as the vision of a prophet, but they are written as straightforward history. The language that is used in these early chapters of Genesis is the same as that which is used in the later ones, when we read about what happened to Abraham, Isaac, Jacob and Joseph.

Furthermore, Professor E. J. Young draws the following conclusion in his monograph *Studies in Genesis One* : 'Genesis one is not poetry or saga or myth, but straightforward, trustworthy

history, and, inasmuch as it is a divine revelation, accurately
records those matters of which it speaks. That Genesis one is
historical may be seen from these considerations: (1) It sustains an
intimate relationship with the remainder of the book. The
remainder of the book (i.e. The Generations) presupposes the
Creation Account, and the Creation Account prepares for what
follows. The two portions of Genesis are integral parts of the book
and complement one another. (2) The characteristics of Hebrew
poetry are lacking. There are poetic accounts of the creation and
these form a striking contrast to Genesis one. (3) The New
Testament regards certain events mentioned in Genesis one as
actually having taken place. We may safely allow the New
Testament to be our interpreter of this mighty first chapter of the
Bible.'[2]

This last point is absolutely crucial. Although we shall be
looking in some detail at the references to Adam in the New
Testament in the next section of this chapter, we shall at this point
consider the attitudes of the Lord Jesus Christ and the New
Testament writers not only to Genesis chapter 1, but also to the
early chapters of Genesis. Did they construe these chapters as
being poetry or myth, or did they accept them as being a literal
account of the creation and early history of the earth?

The Lord Jesus Christ shows that he accepted the early chapters
of Genesis as being literal and historical by his reference to Noah
and the flood: 'As it was in the days of Noah, so it will be at the
coming of the Son of Man. For in the days before the flood, people
were eating and drinking, marrying and giving in marriage, up to
the day Noah entered the ark; and they knew nothing about what
would happen until the flood came and took them all away'
(Matthew 24:37-39). From this passage, and the parallel account
in Luke 17:26-27, it can be seen clearly that the Lord Jesus Christ
regarded the narrative recorded in Genesis chapters 6 to 9 as
historical - he did not consider Noah to be a mythical character nor
did he believe that the flood was a legend.

The fact that the Lord Jesus Christ accepted creation and the
events surrounding Adam and Eve as historical is seen from his
answer to the question, 'Is it lawful for a man to divorce his wife?'
put to him by some Pharisees. Part of his reply was: 'But at the
beginning of creation God "made them male and female". "For this
reason a man will leave his father and mother and be united to his

wife, and the two will become one flesh." So they are no longer
two, but one. Therefore what God has joined together, let man not
separate' (Mark 10:6-9). Intertwined in his answer are two quotations, one from Genesis 1:27 and the other from 2:24.

In the next section we shall be considering in detail the apostle
Paul's arguments which are based on his acceptance of a real
historical Adam. Suffice it to quote just two verses where he
uncompromisingly accepts a historical Adam (and Eve). The first
is 1 Corinthians 15:22: 'For as in Adam all die, so in Christ all will
be made alive,' and the other is 1 Timothy 2:13: 'For Adam was
formed first, then Eve.'

Furthermore, in his sermon given to the Atheneans at a meeting
of the Areopagus, Paul declared God to be the one 'who made the
world and everything in it' and that 'From one man he made every
nation of men' (Acts 17:24, 26).

When we turn to Luke, we find a similar testimony to the literal
truth of Genesis. In Luke's account of the genealogy of the Lord
Jesus Christ via Mary, his mother, his descent from Adam is given
(Luke 3:23-38). Luke accepted the reality and historicity of those
patriarchs who lived before Abraham's time. When Luke came to
Adam, the first man, he was led by the Holy Spirit to record, 'Adam,
the son of God', for such he was in that God had indeed made him
in his own likeness. As pointed out by Professor Versteeg of the
Theological Seminary of the Christian Reformed Churches in the
Netherlands, 'That Adam is called the son of God, as Seth, in turn
is called a son of Adam, is to be regarded as an echo of Genesis 5:1-
3, where we read that God made Adam in the likeness of God, while
Adam begat Seth in his likeness, and his image.'[3]

The beloved disciple John accepted the historicity of the story
of Cain's killing his brother Abel, which is recorded in Genesis 4,
for he wrote, 'Do not be like Cain, who belonged to the evil one and
murdered his brother. And why did he murder him? Because his
own actions were evil and his brother's were righteous' (1 John
3:12).

Finally, the apostle Peter revealed his belief in a literal universal flood when he wrote in his second epistle concerning waters by
which 'the world that then was, being overflowed with water,
perished' (2 Peter 3:6 AV).

The attitude of the Lord Jesus Christ and the New Testament
writers to the early chapters of Genesis shows quite clearly that they

believed that these chapters contained a literal historical account of events. There is not a hint that any one of them considered that the Genesis account of the creation and early history of the earth was in any way poetic, mythical or indeed evolutionary. By taking them as our guide, we are taught what our attitude should be. The early chapters of Genesis contain a true historical record of what actually happened. It is written as history, for it is history.

At this point, I want us to consider for a moment the striking contrast between the Genesis account of the creation and some ancient creation myths.[4] In the Indian creation myth, for example, the earth is flat and triangular and is supported by three elephants, who in turn are supported by a giant turtle swimming in a sea of mercury. In one Egyptian creation myth, the god Atum came into being by himself and then brought forth gods on a primeval hill above the waters of Chaos. Next, he brought forth the world into order and out of the dark deep assigned places and functions to the other deities, including Osiris. In another Egyptian creation myth, the sun-god Ra gained victory over the underworld Apophis, and people were created from Ra's tears, all men being created equal in opportunity to enjoy the basic necessities of life.

In the famous Babylonian creation myth called *Enuma elish,* the young god Marduk, armed with magic spells, succeeded in killing the ocean, who is the goddess Ti'amat, together with her lieutenant, Kingu. Marduk then split Ti'amat's corpse lengthways into two and from one half he made the sky, and from the other half he made the earth; the rivers Tigris and Euphrates flowing from her eyes. Marduk then made man using the blood of Kingu.[5] In another Babylonian creation myth (the Epic of Atrahasis), the gods, who were working digging canals and tilling the soil, went on strike when they decided the work was too hard. The god Enlil, who was the son of Anu, king of heaven, killed the strike leader, mixed his flesh and blood with some clay and made a substitute worker, man. It is often taught that there are similarities between the Babylonian creation myths and the Genesis account of creation, thus demoting the Genesis account to the position of a creation myth. After reading an account of two of the Babylonian creation myths and comparing them with the early chapters of Genesis, readers may draw their own conclusions.

We are left then with the conclusion that Adam and his wife Eve were real individuals, the first human pair, and that they were supernaturally created by God. As such an act is a non-repeatable event, it cannot be subjected to rigorous scientific experimentation and observation. However, as pointed out in the last chapter, the scientific disciplines of comparative anatomy, molecular biology and genetics support the concept of people being the result of such a creative act as described in Genesis. We will be returning to the Genesis account of the life of Adam on a number of occasions in the next few sections, especially in the next one which paradoxically looks at the New Testament teachings about Adam.

Adam in the New Testament

In contrast to the Old Testament, the spiritual aspects of Adam's creation and life are emphasized in the New Testament. This does not mean that Adam is not considered to be a real historical person. Far from it! In fact, the apostle Paul compares and contrasts the Lord Jesus Christ with Adam on a number of occasions. This made Thomas Goodwin, the seventeenth-century President of Magdalen College, Oxford remark: 'In God's sight, there are two men - Adam and Jesus Christ - and these two men have all other men hanging at their girdle strings.'[6]

In particular, I want us to look at three passages where Paul refers to Adam and Jesus Christ. These passages are found in Romans 5, 1 Corinthians 15 and 1 Timothy 2. We will look at them in reverse order.

Giving instruction to Timothy about congregational worship, Paul wrote, 'A woman should learn in quietness and full sub-mission. I do not permit a woman to teach or to have authority over a man; she must be silent' (1 Timothy 2:11-12).

Why does Paul give such an instruction? In the following two verses he gives two reasons by referring to the creation of the first human pair and their subsequent fall into sin. His first reason is 'For Adam was formed first, then Eve' (verse 13), and his second reason is 'And Adam was not the one deceived; it was the woman who was deceived and became a sinner' (verse 14). Here there is a clear reference to the historicity of Adam, Eve and the Fall (more of that later). Paul therefore gave instructions for congregational worship based upon the creation and subsequent fall of the first human pair. This point is further illustrated by considering what Paul wrote to

the Christians in Corinth, when he gives advice about the length of
Christians' hair by referring to the creation of Adam and Eve: 'A
man ought not to have long hair, since he is the image and glory of
God; but the woman is the glory of man. For man did not come
from woman, but woman from man; neither was man created for
woman, but woman for man'[7] (1Corinthians 11:7-9).

Turning to 1 Corinthians 15, we see how Paul compares and
contrasts what we inherit from Adam with that which we can
receive from the Lord Jesus Christ: 'For as in Adam all die, so in
Christ all will be made alive' (1 Corinthians 15:22). Here, in this
one verse we can see the significance that Adam and Christ have for
all human beings. Through Adam and his sin, death came to all.
Through Christ and his resurrection (remember that 1 Corinthians
chapter 15 is about the resurrection), all can be made alive - by
believing on and trusting in the Lord Jesus Christ: that is what is
meant by the words 'in Christ'. No wonder, then, that Paul could
also write, 'So it is written: "The first man Adam became a living
being", the last Adam, a life-giving spirit' (1 Corinthians 15:45).

Paul then continues with his contrast of the first man, Adam,
with the last Adam, Christ, as follows: 'The first man was of the
dust of the earth, the second man from heaven. As was the earthly
man, so are those who are of the earth; and as is the man from
heaven, so also are those who are of heaven. And just as we have
borne the likeness of the earthly man, so shall we bear the likeness
of the man from heaven' (1 Corinthians 15:47-49).

Throughout this chapter, which is my favourite chapter in the
Bible, Paul contrasts that which we naturally inherit from Adam
with that which we can have in Christ. Paul not only believed in a
real Christ, but he believed in a real Adam. To him, Adam was not
a 'teaching model' or myth, but a real historical person.

Finally, in Romans 5, Paul contrasts the fruit of Adam's
disobedience with that of Jesus Christ's obedience in verses 12-19:
'Therefore, just as sin entered the world through one man, and death
through sin, and in this way death came to all men, because all
sinned - for before the law was given, sin was in the world. But sin
is not taken into account when there is no law. Nevertheless, death
reigned from the time of Adam to the time of Moses, even over
those who did not sin by breaking a command, as did Adam, who
was a pattern of the one to come.

'But the gift is not like the trespass. For if the many died by the trespass of the one man, how much more did God's grace and the gift that came by the grace of the one man, Jesus Christ, overflow to the many! Again, the gift of God is not like the result of the one man's sin: The judgement followed one sin and brought condemnation, but the gift followed many trespasses and brought justification. For if, by the trespass of the one man, death reigned through that one man, how much more will those who receive God's abundant provision of grace and of the gift of righteousness reign in life through the one man, Jesus Christ.

'Consequently, just as the result of one trespass was condemnation for all men, so also the result of one act of righteousness was justification that brings life for all men. For just as through the disobedience of the one man the many were made sinners, so also through the obedience of the one man the many will be made righteous.'

I have quoted this rather lengthy passage so that the force of Paul's argument will come across. It is obvious that a belief in a historical Adam is absolutely crucial to the plan of salvation. This has been commented upon: 'The argument of Paul in Romans 5 depends absolutely for its validity on the fact that, as Jesus was an historical Person, so Adam was an historical person. There cannot be a proper parallel between a mythical Adam and an historical Christ. Adam is as essential to the Christian system of theology as Jesus Christ is. Christ is indeed called in Scripture "the second Adam", or "the last Adam". Any theory which tends, as the common form of evolution does, to eliminate Adam as a real historical person, is destructive of Christianity.'[8]

In these passages of Scripture we have been considering, we have read much about Adam's disobedience. But what was Adam's sin? In the Genesis account of the creation of Adam, we read, 'And the Lord God commanded the man, "You are free to eat from any tree in the garden; but you must not eat from the tree of the knowledge of good and evil, for when you eat of it you will surely die"' (Genesis 2:16-17).

In the next chapter, however, we read that Adam and his wife Eve ate this forbidden fruit[9] in complete disobedience to the spoken word of God. Why did they do this? The Bible records that Satan, in the form of a serpent, tempted Eve. He introduced an element of doubt into her mind by questioning what God had said. He also lied to her by telling her that she would not die if she ate the fruit of the tree of the knowledge of good and evil. It was the eating of this fruit, in complete disobedience to God's express command, that is referred to as the Fall and this resulted in many changes taking place within God's creation. Adam's sin therefore was disobeying God.

We have already seen that it was by Adam's disobedience that death (physical as well as spiritual) was introduced onto the scene of time, and that death passed upon everyone - you and me included. Other changes were that the eyes of Adam and Eve were opened so they knew they were naked; woman's sorrow and conception was increased; the ground was cursed; and thorns and thistles began to grow. No wonder the apostle Paul stated, 'For we know that the whole creation groaneth and travaileth in pain together until now' (Romans 8:22 AV). The reversal of the effects of the Fall and the restoration of man to the glory of God is the ultimate object of our salvation, as we shall see in the next chapter.

Having looked at the teachings connected with Adam in the New Testament, we can see clearly that Adam is considered to be a historical person - the first human being. Having established this, I now want us to look at the problems that theistic evolutionists have when they consider the question: 'Who was Adam?'

Adam and theistic evolutionists

The Bible teaches quite clearly that Adam was the first man and that Eve was his wife and that they were both supernaturally made: Adam from the dust of the ground and Eve from Adam's side. Every human being on this planet is therefore descended from this couple. Adam disobeyed God's command, thereby sinning, and as a result all human beings are sinners and all die. Bearing these matters in mind, let us look at what theistic evolutionists believe about Adam and Eve for theistic evolutionists believe in evolution but believe that God has controlled the processes.

From a consideration of the genealogies in Genesis chapters 5 and 11, it is possible to show that it is unlikely that Adam lived more than twenty thousand years ago.[10] Theistic evolutionists are now faced with a number of problems, for according to their views on origins, based upon evolution, Adam would have been a comparatively late arrival on the *Homo sapiens* scene. (Remember that *Homo sapiens* is supposed to have evolved something like a hundred and fifty thousand years ago.) The conservative theistic evolutionist usually interprets Genesis chapters 1 to 3 in the following way: 'The first three chapters of Genesis are a mixture of history and allegory. We cannot take the creation narrative literally, but the New Testament insists on a historical Adam and Eve, and a real Fall. So we must proceed as follows. All forms of life, including *Homo sapiens,* evolved along Darwinian lines. But these naturally-evolved human beings still lacked one vital attribute of true humanity: they were unable to commune with God - they were not yet "religious animals". So God selected one chosen pair from this species, and gave them this missing element of spirituality and a moral law. He remained in close touch with these two for a while, but they failed to keep his commands. God therefore withdrew his presence from them, thus sentencing them to "spiritual death". This punishment has been extended to embrace the whole of mankind, thus making necessary the atoning sacrifice of Christ.'[11]

On the face of it, such an approach accepts the Bible as inspired and authoritative, and the fall of Adam and Eve as a historical fact. Yet there are many problems with this approach; among these are the following:

1. As Adam was the first man, as the Scriptures so emphatically teach, then what is the nature of the people (i.e. the *Homo sapiens*) who lived before Adam? Did these pre-Adamites have souls that could be saved? When did Adam's contemporaries become 'religious animals'?

2. As Adam was the first person to sin, as the Bible records, and as we all inherit sin because we are all descended from Adam, then what about Adam's contemporaries? Were they sinless until Adam sinned? How did they sin? How could they inherit sin from Adam seeing they were not descended from him?

3. As the Bible teaches quite clearly that people die because of Adam's sin, were pre-Adamites immortal? Did Adam's contemporaries start dying when he sinned?

4. As Genesis 3:20 teaches that Eve would be the mother of all human beings, what about those people who were and are descended from Adam's contemporaries? Are these then, by definition 'not human'?

The answers given by theistic evolutionists to such questions may be gleaned by considering the views of Professor R. J. Berry, Professor of Genetics at University College London. He accepts that the New Testament regards Adam as the first parent of the whole human race, but argues that 'It would be incompetent exegesis to regard the Bible's use of "whole human race" as necessarily synonymous with the biological species *Homo sapiens.*'[12] He goes on to state: 'We are human because we have been created in God's image, not because of our membership of a species defined on morphological grounds as *Homo sapiens;* we are qualitatively separable from other hominids not because of any genetical event but because of God's in-breathing.'[13]

Professor Berry also states: 'Humanness does not spread from generation to generation in the same way as physically inherited traits; every individual is uniquely endowed with spiritual life by God. Consequently it is quite possible that, at some time after God had created Adam, he then conferred his image on all members of the same biological species at the time.'[14]

We can see therefore that the main thrust of the theistic evolutionist's argument is that there is a distinction between a member of the species of *Homo sapiens* and a human being. The difference is that being human is the result of the act of God's in-breathing as recorded in Genesis 2:7. Some theistic evolutionists argue that this happened to a member of the species of *Homo sapiens* that had been specially selected for this purpose by God; others believe that Adam was supernaturally created by Almighty God from the dust of the ground at the same time that the species of *Homo sapiens* had evolved and was firmly established on the earth.

We can also see from what Professor Berry believes that theistic evolutionists argue that humanness was conferred on all members of the species of *Homo sapiens* at the same time that Adam lived, or at some short time after. If this were true, then it would mean that those members of the species of *Homo sapiens* who were contemporaries of Adam would not have been descended from him, and furthermore, Eve would not have been their mother. Such views run counter to the clear teachings of Scripture (see Acts 17:26 and Genesis 3:20).

Although E. K. Victor Pearce does not consider himself to be a theistic evolutionist,[15] he nevertheless adopts a theistic evolutionist's approach to the origin of people. As an anthropologist, he believes that the Old Stone Age men were pre-Adamites and that these were the people that God created in Genesis 1:27.[16] He then suggests that Adam was the first New Stone Age farmer in the Middle East. He also has some rather unorthodox beliefs about Satan's fall occurring early in creation in a 'minerallogica era' and that 'It is possible that he [Satan] had caused earlier races to fall.' Such views are difficult to reconcile with the clear teachings of the Scriptures.

We can see then that theistic evolutionists' interpretations of the early chapters of Genesis create more problems than they solve. The reason for this is that theistic evolutionists take a peculiar stance: they believe that the inspired narrative in Genesis chapters 2 and 3 switches from history to allegory (myth) and vice versa without any warning whatsoever. Such an inconsistent interpretation of Genesis inevitably results in confusion, for who decides what is history and what is allegory? Only by accepting a historical Adam and Eve who were the first pair of human beings created by God do we solve all the theological problems.

Adam and the gap theory

The gap theory gets its name from the idea that there is a time gap between Genesis 1:1 and 1:2. This suggestion was first made in 1814 by the famous Dr Thomas Chalmers of the University of Edinburgh. The gap theory maintains that the original earth created in Genesis 1:1 was populated with plants and animals, but because of the fall of Lucifer (Satan) this original creation was destroyed by God by means of a universal cataclysmic flood (called Lucifer's flood). At the same time, the earth was plunged into darkness and *became* 'without form and void' as recorded in Genesis 1:2(AV). The evolutionary geological time-table is supposed to have occurred during this time interval so that the fossils found in the earth's crust are relics of the originally perfect world which was supposedly destroyed *before* the six literal days of creation (or recreation) recorded in Genesis 1:3-31.

Weston Fields in his book *Unformed and Unfilled* has shown the unscriptural basis of the gap theory. Those wishing to study this in more detail are directed towards his excellent treatise.[17] However, I want us to consider some of the problems with the gap theory as it impinges upon Adam.

First of all, let us remind ourselves of what God saw when he had finished creating everything: 'God saw all that he had made, and it was very good' (Genesis 1:31). Now according to the gap theory, Adam was placed as a very late arrival in a world that had recently been destroyed; a world that could scarcely be called 'very good' because it had already become the domain of that fallen, wicked creature, Satan, who is described as 'the god of this world' in 2 Corinthians 4:4(AV).

Furthermore, according to the gap theory, when Adam was created, he would have been literally walking on the graveyard of billions of creatures which had been destroyed in Lucifer's flood, and over which Adam would never exercise dominion. The so-called 'dominion mandate' is recorded in Genesis 1:28, where we read that God said to the first created humans (i.e. Adam and Eve):

'Be fruitful and increase in number;
fill the earth and subdue it.
Rule over the fish of the sea
and the birds of the air
and over every living creature
that moves on the ground.'

It is not only a mandate, but a blessing - it is not only God's commission to subdue the earth but the very bestowal of that function upon humans. It emphasizes the importance of this dominion drive as an attribute of humans who are the image bearers and viceroys of the Creator.

The Bible teaches that death and the 'groaning and travailing in pain' of the present world is the result of Adam's sin (see Romans chapters 5 and 8). The gap theory, however, seriously compromises this biblical doctrine for it teaches that death in the animal kingdom was occurring not only before Adam fell, but long before even Satan rebelled. Some[18] argue that the death that was introduced as a result of Adam's sin was the death of humans and that death in the animal kingdom was already in operation before the Fall. Even if this idea is correct, then there are still problems with the gap theory with the so-called pre-Adamites (i.e. the ones, according to the gap theory, whose fossilized remains we find buried in the sedimentary rocks) living and *dying* before Adam's fall. They would have died not in the same sense that we die, for the gap theory would have us to believe that they were mere animals and that they did not therefore possess an eternal soul.

The gap theory is a recent idea formulated in the last two centuries in an attempt to harmonize creation and evolution. On the face of it, the gap theory appears to offer biblical support for a position that does not radically challenge the evolutionary geological time table. However, when looked at closely, it does not rest upon the impregnable rock of Holy Scripture, for it raises many problems as we consider the biblical teachings about Adam. For example, we saw that it not only compromised the unity and completeness of the Genesis account of the creation, but it also challenges the totality of Adam's dominion and the New Testament teachings of the consequences of Adam's fall.

Adam and fossil people

If we accept that Adam was the first man, then we are led to the inevitable conclusion that every person that has ever lived must have been descended from Adam and his wife, Eve. This includes all the people whose remains we find fossilized, and about whom we read in chapter 3. We have already seen that there is ample evidence from the fossil record that different types of people lived in the past - the habilines, the *Homo erectus* people, the Neanderthals, as well as *Homo sapiens sapiens*. To try to relate these peoples to each other and to Adam is an impossible task at this time, for we have already seen in the last chapter how difficult it is to try to unravel how the various races of people that are on the earth today are related to each other. We can, however, draw one or two tentative conclusions.

Unfortunately, Hollywood has always given us the image of Adam as being a white Caucasian, and Eve as being a fair-haired, fair-skinned beauty. Hence a different image of Adam and Eve may not readily be accepted in the West. However, my own personal view is that Adam (and Eve, for that matter) was probably dark-skinned, with an appearance more like that of *Homo erectus* than that of *Homo sapiens*. Remember we saw in chapter 3 that there is a growing opinion that these two species are one and the same.

My reasons for proffering such a radical view about Adam's appearance are as follows. When considering our ancestors, we must not adopt an evolutionary view of people becoming dark because they were exposed to sunlight, but rather we must realize that Almighty God created the first humans with skin suitable for the conditions he placed them in. Adam's dark skin would therefore have protected him from any harmful rays of the sun, for he lived in a hot sub-tropical climate. We must not forget that the pre-flood water vapour canopy would also have afforded him some protection from the harmful rays of the sun. This view of the colour of Adam's skin is supported by modern research, which indicates that our ancestors were dark-coloured and it is the white varieties of our species that have actually lost out genetically, in that they do not posses the genes to make their skin dark-coloured.

Another reason for holding such a view about Adam's appearance is that the Bible teaches clearly that Adam and his immediate descendants were vegetarians (Genesis 1:29). The jaws of the *Homo erectus* people were generally large and massive with good teeth, which were ideally suited for a vegetarian diet. The brow ridges which we see on the skulls of *Homo erectus* people may have been caused by the same mechanism that causes some modern-day Eskimos to develop brow ridges. Because of the tough food in their diet, Eskimos have to chew their food for a long time. When they are children, this prolonged chewing causes the soft bone of their skull to be pulled and so brow ridges are formed by the strong muscles that develop on the side of the face. These brow ridges must not be thought of in any way as being 'primitive'. The massive jaws of the *Homo erectus* people would have had even stronger jaw muscles than modern-day Eskimos, so it should not surprise us to see even larger brow ridges on the skulls of *Homo erectus* people. We must also remember that the vegetarian diet of the *Homo erectus* people would have been coarse, and should not be compared with our modern vegetarian diets. Such a coarse diet would have taken a lot of chewing.

Conclusion

In this chapter we have considered what the Bible teaches about our forefather, Adam. First of all we saw that the early chapters of

Genesis teach the creation of a real historical pair of humans - Adam and his wife Eve. We considered the interpretation by the New Testament writers and characters to the early chapters of Genesis and we saw that they too held this same view - they considered them to be straightforward history; they did not consider the opening chapters of the book of Genesis to be in any way poetry or myth. We also saw that the spiritual aspects of Adam's creation and life are also emphasized in the New Testament. In particular, that which all human beings inherit because of Adam (i.e. death) is contrasted with that which all people can have in Christ (i.e. abundant eternal life).

We then turned our attention to theistic evolutionists, who rely on evolution for their account of origins and so believe that the inspired narrative in Genesis chapters 2 and 3 switches from history to myth and vice versa without any warning whatsoever. We considered the problems that this causes with the biblical teachings that Adam was the first man and that it was a result of his sin that people die. We saw that we are faced with similar problems when we try to place Adam into the gap theory interpretation of origins.

Finally, we looked briefly at Adam and his relationship with the people whose remains have been fossilized. We had to conclude that these people were descended from him because he is the ancestor of the whole human race. This means that Adam is also our ancestor and that if we traced our family tree back to the beginning, we would arrive at Adam - created perfect by Almighty God, yet one who became a sinner.

7.
Right with God?

Such a book as this would not be complete without a chapter dealing with God's relationship with humans. So far, we have seen that there is no evidence for the evolution of humans from animals. We saw that the evidence from the fossil record as well as evidence from other scientific disciplines does not support this idea. We also saw that the evidence from anatomy, biochemistry and embryology supports the idea that human beings have been designed. Where there is design, there must of necessity be a designer. This designer is the Creator; and this Creator is God.

When we turn to the opening chapters of God's book, the Bible, we read that not only have all life forms been created by God, but all inanimate objects as well. God created everything, including the first human pair - Adam and Eve. Since every human being has descended from this first couple, I want us to consider how God has communicated with the human race. We can read about this in the one book that communicates God's word to us - the Bible.

I have deliberately given this chapter a title which reflects a person's relationship with God, for this is the way that we very often view communication with God. Maybe at this stage you should ask yourself the question: 'Am I right with God?' Only you can answer this truthfully. If you are, well, 'Praise the Lord!' (as they say in some Christian quarters). If, however, you are not right with God, then it is my fervent hope that by the time you reach the end of this particular chapter, you will have found the Lord Jesus Christ to be your Lord and Saviour so that you will then be right with God.

A communicating God

It is true to say that God is incomprehensible - that is, he can never be fully understood - but, at the same time, he is knowable. On the one hand there seems to be no answer to the questions that Isaiah asked:

> 'To whom, then, will you compare God?
> What image will you compare him to?'
>
> (Isaiah 40:18).

And yet we should all be aware of what Jesus said in his prayer to his Father recorded in John 17:3: 'Now this is eternal life: that they may know you, the only true God, and Jesus Christ, whom you have sent.'

Christians have always been aware of these two ideas that are held side by side. The early Christian fathers, for example, spoke of the invisible God as an unbegotten, nameless, eternal, incomprehensible, unchangeable being and, at the same time, confessed that God reveals himself in and through the Lord Jesus Christ, and therefore can be known unto salvation. God can be known, but it is impossible for humans to have a knowledge of him that is exhaustive and perfect in every way. Yet it is possible to obtain a knowledge of God that is perfectly adequate for the realization of the divine purpose in our lives. True knowledge of God can be acquired only from the divine self-revelation (that is God's communicating knowledge of himself to humans) and only to those who accept this with childlike faith. Christianity necessarily presupposes such a knowledge.

We read in the Bible that God has revealed himself via various names, yet the Bible often speaks of the name of God in the singular (for example in the third commandment found in Exodus 20:7). In such instances 'the name' stands for the whole manifestation of God in his relation to his people. The most simple name used in the Old Testament for God is the Hebrew *'El,* and this conveys the meaning of being first, being Lord, and of being strong and mighty. The name *'Adonai* points to God as the almighty Ruler, whereas *Shaddai* and *'El-Shaddai* are used to show that God possesses all power in heaven and on earth. Through the name *Yahweh,* God reveals himself as the God of grace. In the New Testament we find the Greek equivalents of the Old Testament Hebrew names: for *'El* we find *Theos,* which is the most common name for God; *Yahweh* and *'Adonai* are usually rendered *Kurios* ,which is derived from the Greek word *kuros,* meaning power. We also find that *Pater,* meaning father, is also used repeatedly in the New Testament.

What else does the Bible teach about God? One thing we learn as we read the Scriptures is that God has certain properties that are often referred to by theologians as attributes. Some of these are termed incommunicable attributes and include God's self-existence, his immutability, his infinity and his unity. These belong to what might be called the constitutional nature of God. God's other attributes are termed communicable attributes and emphasize his personal nature. They include his spirituality, his intellectual attributes (the knowledge, wisdom and veracity of God), his moral attributes (the goodness, holiness and righteousness of God) and his sovereignty.

What has all this to do with the understanding of our origins? Well, not so very long ago those who studied the natural sciences attempted to relate their findings to God's natural revelation. For example, the science and study of astronomy was seen to be a study of God's handiwork (Psalm 19:1); natural history was seen to be the study of God's creation and design; and the laws of science were seen to be God's laws. Indeed, scientists often dedicated their books and scientific theses to God and some spoke of thinking God's thoughts after him.

It used to be believed (and still is by Christians, for that matter) that the laws of science hold true and are unchanging because of what the Bible teaches about God and about his involvement with his creation: 'The Lord our God, the Lord is one' (Deuteronomy 6:4). 'He is before all things, and in him all things hold together' (Colossians 1:17).

Because God is a unity and because he is involved now in his creation, it follows that there is a unity in the natural order and a unity in the universe. It also follows that the scientists' belief in the unchanging laws of nature is not because a brief 400 years of scientific measurement have shown that there is stability, but because God, who is true, has promised stability. Scientists may not be aware of this, and they may not accept it - but nevertheless it is so.

The concept of the universality of the laws of science is also a concept proposed by Christians because of their acceptance of the nature of God - his unity and his involvement in creation. This concept states that the laws of science that are in operation today were in operation yesterday and will be in operation again tomorrow (that is, the *time* element), and that these laws are in operation throughout the entire universe (that is, the *dimensional* element). If we remove the belief in the one God who is the Creator, then we have the possibility of quite different laws 'out there', and we find ourselves confronted with the space-lords and the time-lords of science fiction. We begin to listen for sounds from outer space and search for UFOs. The universe suddenly becomes a very hostile place in which to live.

We must also be aware that the Bible gives us no reason to believe that God created the world by the same natural laws with which he now sustains it. Hence all attempts to discover or time the origin of the universe and the origin of people are outside the scope of scientific method. The natural laws then and now are probably not the same. The founders of scientific method laid down that *primary causes* (how the world came into being) must be separated from *secondary causes* (how it works now). Scientific method is about secondary causes - we are not competent to enquire into the primary causes. This explains why creationism is anti-evolution in its approach: it keeps showing why evolution is unscientific and cannot therefore be a secondary cause.

Christians also believe that the universe was created by a God of reason. We find reason from beginning to end in the Bible. God argues rationally with humans, for he not only tells us *what* to do, but *why* we should do it. He also teaches cause and effect in human and divine relations. Now belief in a rational universe is part and parcel of scientific method. The reason for this is that the scientists who defined scientific method believed that the Bible was the book of God's words, and they felt that they should examine God's works (that is, the creation) with the same reverence that they studied God's Word. They found reason in the Bible and they argued that they would find reason in nature. And they did! They were able to build up rational systems on the basis of a uniform and orderly creation, They did not try to impose their systems on nature, as ancient philosophers had done; they learnt through the experimental method the ways in which one part of nature relates to another, and so they were able to use all its powers to help the human race.

Before leaving this section I would like us to consider something which baffles the natural thinking scientist and yet which makes a lot of sense to the Christian. Scientists are perplexed by a string of apparent accidents or coincidences that seem just too improbable to dismiss. Many of the familiar structures of the physical world - atoms, life, stars, galaxies - are remarkably sensitive to the precise form of the fundamental laws of physics. So much so that the slightest shift in the values of the parameters that are found in nature would bring about a drastic and catastrophic change in the organization of the cosmos. It seems as though nature's numbers are finely tuned to make the whole cosmos work properly - just as you would expect if you believed in creation and a Creator.

Consider, for example, the structure of the atomic nuclei. The protons and neutrons are bound tightly together by a strong nuclear force. A few percentage reduction would have a catastrophic result. Deuterium with its one proton and one neutron would come unstuck and so the sun (and all the other stars, for that matter) would not be able to burn because deuterium is an important element in its fuel chain. A few percentage increase in the nuclear force would have a worse catastrophic effect for it would be possible for two protons to stick together and this would mean that the universe would be denuded of free protons, with the result that there would be little hydrogen in the universe. If there was no hydrogen, there would be no water in the universe. If there was no hydrogen, there would be no life on earth, for the chemicals that are found in living systems contain hydrogen. If there was no hydrogen, there would be no sun or stars because these use hydrogen as a fuel in order to burn. God in his wisdom, however, created a universe with all the parameters finely balanced so that the earth would be a suitable place for humans to dwell on (Psalm 115:16). No wonder when God saw all that he had created, he pronounced it to be very good (Genesis 1:31).

Human communication

We read that in the Garden of Eden, God and Adam (and Eve)

communicated with each other.[1] It is this ability to communicate via a language that is unique to humans: 'It begins to look, more and more disturbingly, as if the gift of language is the single human trait that marks us all genetically, setting us apart from all the rest of life. Language is, like nest-building or hive-making, the universal and biologically specific activity of human beings. We engage in it communally, compulsively, and automatically. We cannot be human without it; if we were to be separated from it our minds would die, as surely as bees lost from the hive.'[2]

Furthermore, we are born knowing how to use language: 'Under anything like normal circumstances it is virtually impossible to prevent a child's learning to speak. What is more, children master what appears to be one of the most complex intellectual skills with virtually no tuition. From the cacophony of sounds that the infant hears it is able to construct the elements of its native language, so that by the age of five it uses perhaps two thousand words of spoken vocabulary and comprehends at least four thousand: that these words, furthermore, are strung around at least a thousand rules of grammar adds up to a very impressive achievement.'[3]

No other animal can talk. Apes cannot talk because their vocal apparatus cannot produce the wide range of sounds that characterizes a spoken language. However, it is commonly believed that chimpanzees have been taught to communicate via American Sign Language - a system of hand gestures developed for the deaf. The crucial question is: can apes really master the essence of human language - the creation of sentences?

In the late 1960s, a chimpanzee named Washoe was taught to use 132 signs. However, it is believed that such animals are merely mimicking their teachers and have no comprehension of syntax. Their 'speech' does not grow in complexity, nor does it show any signs of spontaneity. The famous linguist, Noam Chomsky of the Massachusetts Institute of Technology, is quoted as saying, 'It's about as likely that an ape will prove to have a language ability as there is an island somewhere with a species of flightless birds waiting for human beings to teach them to fly.'[4]

We may safely conclude that language is species-specific to humans. Animals have the ability to communicate through vocal noises or by other means, but the most important single feature characterizing human language against every known mode of animal communication is its infinite productivity and creativity.

If we are all descended from a single pair of humans who spoke one language, why are there so many different languages in the world today? Where did all the different languages come from? To answer these questions, we must turn to the account of the Tower of Babel episode found in Genesis 11. Here we read that there was a time when everyone spoke the same language - presumably the same language that Adam and Eve spoke. However, the people living in the plain of Shinar (later called Babylonia) decided to build an edifice (the so-called Tower of Babel) that would reach up to heaven. The building of such a skyscraper was not wrong *per se,* but it was the people's motives that were wrong. The reason that they wished to build such a tower was that they wanted to make a name for themselves; in other words, they sought their own glory, not the glory of God.

This angered God, with the result that he put a stop to their building activities by causing the people to speak different languages. They did not speak another language in addition to their own one, but different people spoke totally different languages. They could no longer be united in their purpose now that their language was divided. They could no longer understand each other, so they could not help each other; nor indeed could they employ one another. The outcome of this was that the people stopped building the Tower of Babel and moved away from that area with the result that they were scattered over all the earth taking with them their new languages. It is from these new languages given to the people at the Tower of Babel that all the different languages of the world have derived.

Obviously there is a relationship between languages and nations. We can see this by looking at the genealogy in Genesis 10, which is called 'The Table of Nations'. In this case 'nation' is to be understood not in terms of dominion or kingdom, but in terms of tribe. A survey of conservative commentators leads to a generally consistent, if incomplete, tracing of the names in the table down to present-day populations.[5] For example, the peoples of north-western Europe (that is the British, Dutch, Germans and Scandinavians, and hence a good proportion of the people living in North America today) are descended from Gomer. The Slavic population are descended from Magog, Meshech and Tubal. Madai is the ancestor of the Medes, and the Greeks come from Javan. Other tracings are possible: 'The sons of Ham again are partly located. Cush is associated with Ethiopia, Mizraim is clearly Egypt in biblical usage. Phut is associated with Libya. Some of the descendants of Canaan are listed in connection with the land of Canaan at the time of Moses and Joshua: for example, the Jebusites, Amorites, and Hivites in Genesis 10:16-17 and again in Exodus 3:8. Among the descendants of Shem, Asshur gave his name to Assyria, Lud to Lydia, and Aram to the Arameans or Syrians. Arphaxad is ancestor to Abraham; hence his descendants, the Hebrews, the Ishmaelites, the Midianites, and the Edomites, are from Shem, as are the Moabites and Ammonites who are descended from Abraham's nephew Lot.'[6]

We must not forget that the Table of Nations is written in connection with the Tower of Babel episode. Hence we read that the lines of the human race are divided linguistically as well as geographically and ethnically (Genesis 10:20, 31). We must see the Tower of Babel episode as the time when God caused various peoples to join up with each other, and at the same time separate from other peoples, because of a common language. Because of this God caused the various races of humankind to develop. I do not believe that it was by chance that the various races of people ended up in their geographical positions, ideally suited to live in those areas. Rather this was the hand of the Lord God guiding them.

For what purpose should we use our language? You will recall that we have already mentioned that Adam communicated with God in the Garden of Eden. This, I believe, should be our prime use of our language - to communicate with God. The Westminster Shorter Catechism asks the question: 'What is the chief end of man?' and gives the answer: 'Man's chief end is to glorify God, and to enjoy him for ever.' The psalmist David expressed this almost three thousand years ago when he wrote, 'I will bless the Lord at all times; his praise shall continually be in my mouth' (Psalm 34:1 AV).

This should be our testimony. God has given us the ability of language so that we can praise him and communicate with him, as well as communicate with each other.

Noah and the flood

What I want us to do in this section is to consider the relationship that Noah had with God. Noah was a person who lived before the

Tower of Babel episode, and, as we shall see, he had a very special relationship with God. In order to find out about the world that Noah lived in, we need to read the early chapters of Genesis. Genesis 4 gives us a glimpse of life in the antediluvian world, into which Noah was born. This brief biblical record is the only fully reliable account that we have of this antediluvian age, for this human civilization was destroyed by the great flood and practically nothing remains of it. The only survivors of this flood were Noah, his wife, their three sons and their three daughters-in-law.

It is obvious from what is written in the early chapters of Genesis that God not only revealed himself, but also his will, to Adam's descendants. For example, Abel, Adam and Eve's second son, is called righteous, and also described as a prophet by the Lord Jesus Christ (Matthew 23:35; Luke 11:50-51). This can only mean that Abel was a man to whom God had not only revealed himself, but also his Word. Presumably because he was a prophet, he would have preached the Word of God by divine enablement.

Abel was, however, killed by his older brother, Cain. One of the questions that is often asked about Cain is 'Where did he get his wife?' Cain, the son of Adam and Eve, was a first generation human, so to speak, and yet the Bible records that he had a wife and children. The simple answer to the question is that he married one of his sisters. In this first generation, all marriages would have been brother-sister marriages: 'In that early time, there were no mutant genes in the genetic systems of any of these children, so that no genetic harm could have resulted from close marriages. Many, many generations later, during the time of Moses, such mutations had accumulated to the point where such unions were genetically dangerous, so that incest was thenceforth prohibited in the Mosaic laws.'[7]

As time went on, the population increased and so did the technology and culture. Metal tools and implements were available to produce what might be called creature comforts. Musical instruments were made and developed to stimulate the emotional and aesthetic senses. People began to live in cities and to produce their food by agricultural means. The people were certainly writing for there is strong evidence that the early chapters of Genesis were written on clay tablets.[8] From our reading about life in this antediluvian age, there does not appear to be any organized system of laws or government for controlling human conduct. This is borne out by the fact that there came a time when the wickedness was so great that God regretted the fact that he had created humans (Genesis 6:6) and so he decided to destroy the whole human race as well as the animals that lived on the earth. We are told, however, that a man named Noah 'found grace in the eyes of the Lord' (Genesis 6:8 AV).

Noah is one of the Old Testament characters who is named in the roll of the faithful in Hebrews 11. In verse 7 of this chapter we read about Noah, who 'when warned about things not yet seen, in holy fear built an ark to save his family. By his faith he condemned the world and became heir of the righteousness that comes by faith.' But what is faith? We spent a whole section in chapter 3 considering the faith of the evolutionist, so we should by now have an idea of what faith is. However, in spite of all that has ever been written about faith, no one has ever put it more concisely than the writer of the book to the Hebrews when he wrote, 'Now faith is the substance of things hoped for, the evidence of things not seen' (Hebrews 11:1 AV).

Commenting on the two strands in this verse, the great Bible commentator Matthew Henry says of faith that 'It is a firm persuasion and expectation that God will perform all he has promised' and that it 'demonstrates to the mind the reality of things that cannot be discerned by the bodily eye'. It is this type of faith that Noah manifested.

We are told that Noah was warned about things not seen. Up until this time there had never been a flood. Apparently, it had never even rained before, for the earth was watered only by a mist (AV) or streams (NIV) (Genesis 2:5-6). It is hard to imagine there being no rain - especially if, like me, you live in Wales! Try to imagine for a moment a world where rain - those little drops of water that fall down from the sky - is unknown. How would you describe rain in such circumstances? There is a delightful story of a little girl in Australia who, because of a prolonged drought, was eight years old before she saw a drop of rain. When the first drops fell as the terrible drought broke, the frightened child went running to her mother crying, 'The water-hole is falling down!'[9]

So why did Noah believe in rain and in a world-wide deluge? Simply because he believed the word of God. It was going to rain; no doubt about it, for God had said so. Presumably the waters above the sky (Genesis 1:7) were somehow or other going to collapse. But it was not just rain that God was going to send, but 'a flood of waters upon the earth, to destroy all flesh' (Genesis 6:17 AV). In other words, Noah believed that there was going to be a judgement. This flood caused many of the sedimentary rocks with their fossils in them to be deposited. Fossils should therefore remind us of this judgement.

Now faith is belief in action. Noah believed God and, as a result, Noah 'in holy fear built an ark to save his family' (Hebrews 11:7). The apostle James challenges us to show our faith by our works. Noah's faith was demonstrated by his actions, and he certainly showed the world that he believed God. For about a hundred and twenty years he organized the building of the ark, which was about 140 metres long, 23 metres wide and 13.5 metres high. The ark was not a small canal barge, such as you often see depicted in children's story books, but it was a large ocean-going vessel with a gross tonnage of almost 14,000 tons.

In Hebrews 11:7 we read that by his faith Noah condemned the world. This he did both by the action of his faith in obeying God's command (in contrast to the ungodly people around and about him), and by his faithful preaching to them, calling them to repentance, denouncing their unbelief, and warning them about the impending judgement of God. No wonder the Bible teaches that Noah was a preacher of righteousness (2 Peter 2:5), for Noah preached the Word of God to the people of his day. He told them of the coming judgement and the way they could be saved by entering the ark. We see then that Noah's faith was not a sweet innocuous fluff. Noah was in a sinful world and he knew that it was meaningless to preach the good news of salvation without the bad news of judgement.

We also read in Hebrews 11:7 that Noah 'became heir of the righteousness that comes by faith'. It is surprising how many believe that believers in the Old Testament were justified by their works, while believers in the New Testament are justified by their faith (and are thus *without* works?). However, the whole point about what is written about Noah, and indeed about what is written about other Old Testament believers in Hebrews 11 is that the saving faith of the believer in both Testaments is identical. In fact, we are exhorted to emulate the Old Testament believers! It was through faith that Noah *inherited* righteousness, and as pointed out by David Chilton in an article 'Faith and Life' in a *Chalcedon*

Report, 'It is not said that he had an experience, but that a legal act was performed on his behalf. Noah was justified by faith. And having true faith, he was obedient to every word of God. Noah did not confuse justification with sanctification by trying to merit God's grace by works; but he knew also that God's justifying grace produces works. Just as justification and sanctification must not be confused, neither may they be separated.'[10]

The writer to the Hebrews not only exhorts us to consider faithful Noah, but also other faithful characters in the Old Testament. After considering a long list of these, however, he tells us to 'fix our eyes on Jesus, the author and perfecter of our faith' (Hebrews 12:2). This is what I want us to do in the next section.

The Lord Jesus Christ

In an earlier section we considered how the various nations originated. God chose one small nation, Israel, to which and through which to reveal himself, and it was into the nation of Israel that the Lord Jesus Christ was born. It was no ordinary conception - the Lord Jesus Christ was conceived by the Holy Spirit and born of the virgin Mary, for he was the Son of God. As the Rev. Rousas Rushdoony points out in an article entitled 'The Magnificat',[11] the Nativity story is often offensive to people because 'It asserts as history an unprecedented "violation" of every premise in the mind of "natural" or fallen man. A virgin conceives, something no virgin is supposed to do, and miraculously so. Added to that upsetting fact is the declaration that the virgin's child "shall be great, and shall be called the Son of the Highest, and the Lord God shall give unto him the throne of his father David" to rule a kingdom of which "there shall be no end" (Luke 1:32-33).' Be that as it may, the Bible is very dogmatic concerning the fact that the Lord Jesus Christ had a miraculous conception and came to this earth to accomplish a specific purpose.

The Lord Jesus Christ was born in Bethlehem, and after a period of time in Egypt, his mother and her husband Joseph took him to live in Nazareth where he grew up and 'increased in wisdom and stature, and in favour with God and man' (Luke 2:52 AV). Now one of the startling differences between the Lord Jesus Christ and every other single person that has ever lived is that he was sinless.

The writer to the Hebrews says that he 'was in all points tempted like as we are, yet without sin' (Hebrews 4:15 AV). This is a remarkable statement and is worth considering carefully. We are all aware that we sin. There is not one person reading this book that can say that he or she has never sinned. Yet the Bible categorically asserts that the Lord Jesus Christ never sinned. There is not one other single person who has ever lived of whom this can truthfully be said.

You may think that people sin because of their circumstances and that if everything were perfect, then there would not be any sin. This is not what the Bible teaches. The first human pair lived in a perfect world in the paradise of the Garden of Eden - and yet they sinned! Satan, disguised as a serpent, tempted Eve with the fruit of the tree of the knowledge of good and evil. In Genesis 3:6 we read that Eve saw that the fruit was 'good for food and pleasing to the eye, and also desirable for gaining wisdom'. The apostle John, commenting on what is in the world (in contrast with what God has to offer), uses a similar phraseology in 1 John 2:16: 'the lust of the flesh, and the lust of the eyes, and the pride of life' (AV). Interestingly, when Satan came to the Lord Jesus Christ, he had nothing new with which to tempt him, as we shall see.

The first temptation was to turn stones into bread. Remember how Eve had seen that the fruit was good for food and how John wrote about the lust of the flesh? Adam and Eve could eat of any fruit in the garden except the fruit of this one tree. In contrast, Jesus had been in the wilderness and had been fasting for forty days and forty nights. Adam and Eve did not resist temptation - they ate the forbidden fruit. In contrast, the Lord Jesus Christ resisted temptation by quoting Scripture (Deuteronomy 8:3) and did not sin.

In another temptation, the Lord Jesus Christ was shown all the kingdoms of the world at a glance. Remember how Eve had seen that the fruit was pleasing to the eye and how John wrote about the lust of the eyes? The temptation was for Jesus to get these *without* suffering; to get the crown without the cross. One day the Lord Jesus Christ will inherit all the kingdoms of the world (Revelation 11:15), but in order to do so, he had to die a cruel death on Calvary. In contrast to Adam and Eve, the Lord Jesus Christ again resisted temptation (by again quoting Scripture, this time from Deuteronomy 6:13) and was without sin.

In a further temptation, Satan took the Lord Jesus Christ to a high pinnacle. According to the New Testament commentator William Hendriksen, this may have been the roof edge of Herod's royal portico overhanging the Kedron Valley at a height of some 135 metres.[12] This time, Satan quotes Scripture (Psalm 91:11-12). Here there is a slight hint of 'Hath God said...?' which is what Satan first said to Eve in the Garden of Eden. This temptation was a false trust in the Father risking self-destruction. It can also be compared with what Eve thought about the forbidden fruit when she saw that it was desirable for gaining wisdom. We can see this comparison in terms of the temptation for the Lord Jesus Christ to gain instant spiritual wisdom. We can also see the temptation of spiritual pride - to be under the special protection of holy angels. Again there is a link with the pride of life about which the apostle John wrote in 1 John 2:16. The Lord Jesus Christ resisted this temptation also (by once more quoting a passage of Scripture from the book of Deuteronomy, this time from chapter 6:16) and so remained sinless.

Now the main purpose of God's intervention into human affairs (so to speak) was to procure salvation for people. To do this, the sinless Son of God not only had to die on the cross on Calvary, but on that same cross, he who knew no sin had to be made to be sin for us (2 Corinthians 5:21). The apostle Peter expressed the same thought when he wrote that Jesus himself bore our sins in his body on the tree (1 Peter 2:24). Here the sinless Jesus Christ became sin and was sacrificed for us - so that our sins could be forgiven us. This then is the good news (the gospel): sin, which places a barrier between God and humans has been dealt with by God, for 'the blood of Jesus Christ his Son cleanseth us from all sin' (1 John 1:7 AV).

This then is *the* way back to God - in and through the Lord Jesus Christ, God's only begotten Son. No wonder the Lord Jesus Christ could say, 'I am the way and the truth and the life. No one comes to the Father except through me' (John 14:6).

But the Lord Jesus did not stay dead after his crucifixion, but on the third day he rose from the dead. *Jesus is alive!* The Bible also teaches that he ascended into heaven. No wonder then that the writer to the Hebrews wrote, 'Therefore he is able to save completely [or for ever (footnote)] those who come to God through

him, because he always lives to intercede for them' (Hebrews 7:25)
and 'How shall we escape if we ignore such a great salvation?'
(Hebrews 2:3).

Just before his ascension, the Lord Jesus Christ gave the great
commission to his disciples: 'Therefore go and make disciples of
all nations, baptizing them in the name of the Father and of the Son
and of the Holy Spirit, and teaching them to obey everything I have
commanded you' (Matthew 28:19-20). He then gave this wonderful promise: 'And surely I am with you always, to the very end of
the age' (Matthew 28:20).

What I want us to do in the next section is to consider the future
and in particular to look at what will happen at the very end of the
age.

Have we a future?

I was born towards the end of what is called the Second World War.
Before I was one year old, atomic bombs had been dropped on
Hiroshima and Nagasaki, and before I had completed my secondary education the hydrogen bomb had been 'successfully tested'.
What with the Cold War, the Arms Race, the wars and the rumours
of war, the revolutions and counter-revolutions, the *coups* and
counter-*coups* that have occurred throughout my life, it is true to
say that I have lived all of my life in a world which has been on the
brink of annihilation. This has led a number of people to ponder the
future of the human population of this planet. Indeed, many have
wondered if there is any future at all. The humanist and philosopher
Bertrand Russell wrote a book in the 1950s with the poignant title
Has Man a Future? He saw the most agonizing question of our era
as 'Can man hope to survive a nuclear war?' and he answered it by
suggesting that the human race's only hope is to be found in world
government.

During the latter half of this century, a number of Christians
have also become prophets of doom and have confidently predicted
the imminent return of the Lord Jesus Christ. These Christians have
usually held the pre-millennial view of the second coming of the
Lord Jesus Christ. In other words they believe that the Lord Jesus
Christ will return *before* his millennial reign. They interpret the
book of Revelation as a politico-economic commentary on

Western civilization in the twentieth century, and some have made some extraordinary predictions concerning the immediate future. It is not my intention in this book to expound the errors of such predictions. What I want us to do is to look at what the Bible clearly teaches about the Lord's second coming. Thereby I hope that it will fill our hearts with comfort and also with a fair amount of excitement.

The Bible teaches that we have been living in the last days ever since the Lord Jesus Christ was on the earth (Hebrews 1:1-2) and so theoretically at least this means that the Lord Jesus Christ could return to this earth at any time. The book of Revelation is not a politico-economic commentary about the Western world in the twentieth century, but it was written to first-century Christians in the churches in Asia in order to comfort them at that time. It was not only a comforting book for first-century Christians to read, but it also contains much to comfort twentieth-century Christians, for it tells us that Jesus is victorious, that Satan is defeated, and that the Lord Jesus Christ is coming again!

One thing is very clear and that is that the second coming of the Lord Jesus Christ is a time of judgement - this is the theme of the Old Testament prophets as well as the writers of the New Testament. The Lord Jesus Christ likens this judgement to a shepherd separating sheep from goats (Matthew 25:31-46). In this picture the Christians are likened to sheep who are put on the right-hand side of the shepherd and who receive their inheritance, which is eternal life in the kingdom prepared for them since the creation of the world. The non-Christians, however, are depicted as goats who are placed on the left-hand side of the shepherd, and who then have the following pronouncement made upon them: 'Depart from me, you who are cursed, into the eternal fire prepared for the devil and his angels.' In contrast to the Christians who inherit eternal life, the non-Christians receive eternal punishment on the day of judgement.

Now many people do not like this idea of there being a judgement at which non-Christians will be punished eternally. Indeed, some Christians have argued that the punishment endured by the damned will not endure for ever, but that after a time of punishment in hell, non-Christians will be annihilated. However, this is not what the Bible teaches, for the clear teaching of the Scriptures is that the punishment of unbelievers in hell will continue for ever and ever.[13] Just as God and heaven are eternal, so hell will also be eternal.

In the book of Revelation we read that John had a vision of all the people who have ever lived standing before God's judgement throne (Revelation 20:11-15). In this vision, John saw that books were opened and that those whose names were not written in the book of life were thrown into hell. Those whose names are written in the book of life are the Christians. Interestingly, we read in the book of Revelation that their names are written in the book of life since the creation of the world (Revelation 17:8). Although this doctrine of predestination is clearly taught in Scripture, the responsibility is upon each one of us to repent of our sins and believe on the Lord Jesus Christ for our salvation in and through his blood which he shed on that cruel cross on Calvary.

Just as those who entered the ark in the days of Noah were saved from destruction in the great flood, so those who are in Christ at the time of the end will be saved from the torment of hell. After the flood, God promised never again to destroy the earth with a flood (Genesis 9:11). This was God's covenant with Noah, and the sign of this covenant is the rainbow. However, the Bible teaches that one day, not only the earth, but the entire universe will be destroyed *by fire:* 'But the day of the Lord will come like a thief. The heavens will disappear with a roar; the elements will be destroyed by fire, and the earth and everything in it will be burned up [footnote]... That day will bring about the destruction of the heavens by fire, and the elements will melt in the heat' (2 Peter 3:10, 12). Peter then goes on to say in the next verse that 'We are looking forward to a new heaven and a new earth, the home of righteousness', and this is what the apostle John saw in a vision which is recorded for us in Revelation 21:1: 'Then I saw a new heaven and a new earth, for the first heaven and the first earth had passed away.'

It is at this time that God will restore humans to the perfect glorious position that Adam and Eve had in the Garden of Eden before the Fall. This plan is referred to as God's new creation; it began with salvation and will be complete when God makes all things new.

Although those who are redeemed are referred to as God's new creation in 2 Corinthians 5:17, as yet, however, there is not a full restoration of the original creation. Christians possess only a 'guaranteeing deposit' of it (Ephesians 1:14); they have only *tasted*

of the powers of the world to come (Hebrews 6:5 AV) for the
fulness is yet to come. Although Christians can rejoice in the hope
of the glory of God (Romans 5:2) and although they can experience
a progressive restoration even now to it (2 Corinthians 3:18), the
full unveiling into the full liberty of the glory of God is yet to come
(Romans 8:18-23). The regeneration of the Holy Spirit (Titus 3:5)
which the Christian has already experienced is a foretaste of the
regeneration which is yet to come (Matthew 19:28). The creation
will only be restored to its former glory when God creates a new
heaven and a new earth, and then will be fulfilled the visions of
Isaiah:

'The wolf will live with the lamb,
    the leopard will lie down with the goat,
the calf and the lion and the yearling together;
    and a little child will lead them.
The cow will feed with the bear,
    their young will lie down together,
    and the lion will eat straw like the ox.
The infant will play near the hole of the cobra,
    and the young child put his hand into the
        viper's nest.
They will neither harm nor destroy
    on all my holy mountain,
for the earth will be full of the knowledge of the Lord
    as the waters cover the sea.'

                                       (Isaiah 11:6-9).

and
'"The wolf and the lamb will feed together,
    and the lion will eat straw like the ox,
    but dust will be the serpent's food.
They will neither harm nor destroy
    in all my holy mountain,"
             says the Lord.'

                                     (Isaiah 65:25).
At last the glory of the Lord will once again fill the whole earth:
'For the earth will be filled with the knowledge of the glory of
the Lord, as the waters cover the sea' (Habakkuk 2 :14).
    Many scoff at the idea that the Lord Jesus Christ will come

again, as was predicted by the apostle Peter: 'You must understand that in the last days scoffers will come, scoffing and following their own evil desires. They will say, "Where is this 'coming' he promised? Ever since our fathers died, everything goes on as it has since the beginning of creation"' (2 Peter 3:3-4). In this chapter, Peter deals with the scoffers who ridicule the promise of the second coming of the Lord Jesus Christ. They are those people who do not believe in catastrophism, for their philosophy is summed up as 'Everything goes on as it has since the beginning of creation.' This is the philosophy of the evolutionist and it is called uniformitarianism. It can be summed up in the Hutton's catch-phrase: 'The present is the key to the past.' Peter, however, says that those who ridicule the idea of the Lord's return are ignorant because they are unaware that God did not use uniformitarian processes in the great flood which caused the world that then was to perish, and neither will he use uniformitarian processes at his second coming.

We can imagine the scoffers of Noah's day saying, 'Rain! What's that? Little drops of water falling out of the sky! You've got to be joking. Don't you realize that the earth is watered by mists and streams? It has never rained since the creation and it never will rain.' Can you imagine the jokes about 'Noah's Folly' as he laboured for about 120 years constructing the ark? Those who scoffed all perished in the great flood.

It should not really surprise us that people scoff at the second coming of the Lord Jesus Christ. I remember telling a physicist that the Bible teaches that the Lord Jesus Christ will return on clouds. At once he started to ridicule the whole idea of there being a heaven and of the Lord Jesus Christ coming to this planet from 'outer space' and descending to the earth on clouds. He waxed eloquent about the astronomers' latest ideas about the nature of the universe and of how such an event was impossible! He mocked at the idea of the Lord returning in clouds. Those who mocked at the idea of the great flood and did not repent were judged at the time of the great flood. Similarly, those who scoff at the idea of the second coming of the Lord Jesus Christ and do not repent will be judged at his coming. I trust that you are not one of the scoffers, and that you are prepared to meet your Maker on that day.

Conclusion

In this chapter we have considered God's dealings with the human race. First we considered who God is and how he reveals himself to us both through his written Word and also through his works (the creation). We then considered how we communicate with each other through the remarkable gift of language. We also considered the origin of the world's many different languages and saw that this is tied up with the origins of the various races.

We then considered how God revealed himself and his Word to Noah and how by faith he acted upon God's command so that he and his family were saved from the great flood by entering the ark that Noah had built. We saw the effect of Noah's faith on him and his family (who were saved) and on the rest of the world (who were damned). We were also reminded that Noah was a preacher of righteousness and that he did not let the people of his day meet their end without their being warned of the coming judgement: the cataclysmic flood that was to destroy all flesh.

We then looked at the greatest Israelite who has ever lived, the Lord Jesus Christ - the second Adam. We saw that he had a miraculous conception for he was the Son of God. The main purpose of his sinless life and his death was so that he could save people from their sins. The sinless Son of God was made sin for us on Calvary's cross with the result that anyone who believes on him shall not perish, but have everlasting life. But Jesus is not dead, for he rose from the dead. He is alive! And he is coming again. This is the Christian's glorious hope.

In this age of bad news, we can look forward with hope to the future - to the second coming of the Lord Jesus Christ. The Lord Jesus Christ will return one day to judge the whole human race, and on that day he will make a new heaven and earth and the whole creation will be restored perfectly by him. Just as this new creation will not be a cosmic accident, so the first creation, including the creation of our ancestors, Adam and Eve, was not the result of chance natural processes, but it was carefully planned and designed by Almighty God. We have seen in this book that the scientific evidence from the various scientific disciplines at which we have looked (these include anatomy, biochemistry, embryology and palaeontology), fully supports this idea, and we are forced to conclude that far from being a cosmic accident, humans are fearfully and wonderfully made.

References

Chapter 1

1. Quoted in 'Julian Sorell Huxley' by J. R. Baker FRS in *Biographical Memoirs of Fellows of the Royal Society*, published by the Royal Society in November 1976.
2. Richard Spilsbury, *Providence Lost - A Critique of Darwinism* (Oxford University Press, 1974), p.120.
3. 'At Random' a television preview on 21 November 1959 in *Tax*, vol. 3, (1960), pp.41-65.
4. See for example D. B. Kitts, 'Palaeontology and Evolutionary Theory', *Evolution*, vol. 28, (1974), p.466.
5. Quoted in, 'Are the Reports of Darwin's Death Exaggerated?' by Brian Leith in *The Listener*, vol. 106, No. 2730 (8 October 1981), p.390.
6. *A Surgeon Looks at Evolution*, quoted in the Evolution Protest Movement pamphlet No. 223 (January 1980).
7. *What's this Humanism?* published by the British Humanist Association.
8. Nigel M. de S. Cameron, 'Why Evolution Must Stay on the Agenda', *Evangelicals Now* (September 1986), p.9.
9. John 3:16
10. Laura Lederer, ed., *Take Back the Night: Women on Pornography*, (Bantam, 1982).
11. When a baby is dedicated in the church where I am a member, the Church Secretary gives a copy of the Bible to its parents informing them that it is the Maker's Instructions.
12. Psalm 139:14.

Chapter 2

1. I have given a conservative figure; some evolutionists believe it could be as much as twenty thousand million.
2. This number is Freeman Dyson's Number and is written as $10^{10^{76}}$. It is the figure one followed by 10^{76} zeros. Now 10^{76} is the figure one followed by seventy-six zeros. The number of zeros in Freeman Dyson's Number is so great as to be almost unimaginable, for if three hundred thousand million billion zeros (i.e. 3×10^{23} zeros) were typed every hundred thousand millionth of a billionth of a second (i.e. 10^{-23} seconds), it would take over ten thousand million billion years (i.e. 10^{22} years) to type all the zeros in this number! (In this calculation, I have used the British billion which is a million million rather than the American billion which is only a thousand million.)

3. Ozone is, of course, an allotrope of oxygen.

Chapter 3
1. See for example: Paul M. Steidl, *The Earth, the Stars and the Bible*, (Presbyterian & Reformed, 1979); Harold S. Slusher, *The Origin of the Universe*, (Institute for Creation Research, San Diego, 1978); Harold S. Slusher and Stephen J. Duursma, *The Age of the Solar System*, (Institute for Creation Research, San Diego, 1978).
2. See for example: S.E.Aw, *Chemical Evolution*, (Master Books, San Diego, 1982); A. E. Wilder Smith, *He Who Thinks Has To Believe*, (Master Books, San Diego, 1981); A. J. Monty White, *What About Origins?* (Dunestone Printers, Newton Abbot, 1978), pp.77-94.
3. Duane T. Gish, *Evolution: The Challenge of the Fossil Record*, (Master Books, San Diego, 1985).
4. Francis Hitching, *The Neck of the Giraffe* (Pan, London, 1982).
5. Gish, *Evolution: The Challenge of the Fossil Record*, p.229.
6. Hitching, *Neck of the Giraffe*, p.17.
7. Charles Darwin, *The Origin of Species* (Penguin Books, 1968), p.291.
8. Darwin, *Origin of Species*.
9. D. V. Ager, *Proceedings of the Geologists' Association*, vol. 89 (part 1) (1978), p.100.
10. D. B. Kitts, 'Palaeontology and Evolutionary Theory', *Evolution*, vol. 28 (1974), p.466.
11. R. E. Kofahl and K. L. Segraves, *The Creation Explanation* (Harold Shaw, Illinois, 1975), p.44.
12. Quoted by Norman Macbeth, *Darwin Retried* (Delta, New York, 1971), p.127.
13. Sidney W. Fox, 'Origins of Biological Information and the Genetic Code', *Molecular and Cellular Biochemistry*, vol. 3 (1974), pp.129-142.
14. Daniel I. Axelrod, "Early Cambrian Marine Fauna", *Science*, vol. 128 (1958), pp.7-9.
15. F. D. Ommaney, *The Fishes* in *Life Nature Library* (Time-Life, New York, 1964), p.60.
16. Gish, *Evolution: The Challenge of the Fossil Record*, p.69.
17. Hans Fricke, 'Coelacanths: The Fish That Time Forgot', *National Geographic*, vol. 173 (June 1988), pp.824-838.
18. Gish, *Evolution: The Challenge of the Fossil Record*, p.77.
19. Gish, *Evolution: The Challenge of the Fossil Record*, pp.96-97.
20. A. S. Romer, *Vertebrate Paleontology* (University of Chicago Press, Chicago & London, 3rd. Edition, 1966), p.303.
21. Article 'Mammalia' in *Encyclopaedia Britannica* in *Macropaedia*, vol. 11 (15th. Edition, 1977), p.414.
22. G. Gamow and M. Ycas, *Mr Tomkins Inside Himself* (Allen & Unwin, London, 1968), p.149.
23. Gish, *Evolution: The Challenge of the Fossil Record*, pp.130-228.
24. *Our Fossil Relatives* (British Museum [Natural History], London, 1983), p.6.
25. Richard E. Leakey, *The Making of Mankind* (Michael Joseph Ltd., London, 1981), p.43.
26. A. J. Kelso, *Physical Anthropology* (J. P. Lippincott, New York, 2nd Edition, 1974), p.142.

27. Kenneth F. Weaver, 'The Search for Our Ancestors', *National Geographical*, vol. 168 (number 5), (November 1985), pp.560-623.
28. A. W. Mehlert, 'Lucy - Evolution's Solitary Claim for An Ape/Man - Her Position is Slipping Away', *Creation Research Society Quarterly*, vol. 22 (no. 3) (December 1985), pp.144-145.
29. A. Walker and R. E. F. Leakey, 'The hominids of East Turkana', *Scientific-American*, vol. 239 (1978), pp.44-56.
30. Weaver, 'Search for Our Ancestors', p.600.
31. Weaver, 'Search for Our Ancestors', pp.610-612.
32. P. Andrews, 'The Descent of Man', *New Scientist*, vol. 102 (1984), p.25.
33. See for example, L. B. Halstead, *Hunting The Past*, (Book Club Associates, 1982), pp.162-163.
34. A. G. Thorne and P. G. Macumber, *Nature*, vol. 238 (1972), p.316. Also reported in 'Last Adam' in *Scientific American*, vol. 222 (October 1972), p.48.
35. C. B. Stringer, F. C. Howell and J. K. Melentis, 'The Significance of the Fossil Hominid Skull from Petralona, Greece', *Journal of Archaeological Science*, vol. 6 (1979), pp.235-253.
36. Richard Leakey and Alan Walker, '*Homo erectus* Unearthed', *National Geographic*, vol. 168 (November 1985), pp.625-629.
37. 'Use of Symbols Antedates Neanderthal Man', *Science Digest*, vol. 73 (March 1973), p.22.
38. Halstead, *Hunting The Past*, p.173.
39. David M. Raup, 'Conflicts Between Darwin and Palaeontology', *Bulletin*, Field Museum of Natural History, vol. 50 (January 1979).
40. Ernst Mayr, *Animal Species and Evolution* (Belknap Press of Harvard University Press, Massachusetts, 1963).
41. Mark Ridley, 'Evolution and Gaps in the Fossil Record', *Nature*, vol. 286 (31 July 1980), p.444.
42. D. V. Ager, 'The Nature of the Fossil Record', *Proceedings of the Geologists' Association*, vol. 87 (part 2) (1976), pp.131-159. (This article is a record of the Presidential Address delivered on 5 March 1976.)
43. Ridley, *Evolution and Gaps in the Fossil Record*.
44. Reviewed in Ridley, *'Evolution and Gaps in the Fossil Record'*.
45. Richard Leakey and Roger Lewin, *Origins* (Futura, Macdonald & Co., London, 1982), p.75.

Chapter 4

1. Quoted by Malcolm Bowden, *Ape-Man - Fact or Fallacy?* (Sovereign, Bromley, 1981, 2nd edition), pp.58-59.
2. A. J. E. Cave and W. L. Straus Jr, 'Pathology and Posture of Neanderthal Man', *Quarterly Review of Biology*, vol. 32 (1957), pp.348-363.
3. Bowden, *Ape-man - Fact or Fallacy?*, p.58.
4. Bowden, *Ape-man - Fact or Fallacy?*
5. Bowden, *Ape-man - Fact or Fallacy?*, pp.46-47.
6. Richard Leakey and Roger Lewin, *Origins* (Futura, MacDonald & Co., London & Sydney, 1982), p.85.
7. Arthur V. Chadwick, 'Of Dinosaurs and Men', *Origins*, vol. 14 (1) (1987), pp.33-40.
8. Chadwick, 'Of Dinosaurs and Men'.
9. Chadwick, 'Of Dinosaurs and Men'.

10. B. R. Neufeld, 'Dinosaur Tracks and Giant Men', *Origins*, vol. 2 (1975), pp.64-76.
11. G.Kuban, 'The Taylor Site "Man-Tracks"', *Origins Research*, vol.9 (Spring/ Summer 1986), pp.1-10, and R. Hastings, 'New Observations on Paluxy Tracks Confirm Their Dinosaurian Origin', *Journal of Geological Education*, vol. 35 (1987), pp.4-15.
12. Chadwick, 'Of Dinosaurs and Men'.
13. John Morris, *Tracking Those Incredible Dinosaurs* (CLP, San Diego, 1980), p.191.
14. John Morris, 'The Paluxy River Mystery', ICR *Impact* No.151 (January 1986).
15. Chadwick, 'Of Dinosaurs and Men'.
16. See for example David H. Milne and Steven D. Schafersman, 'Dinosaur Tracks, Erosion Marks and Midnight Chisel Work (But No Human Footprints) in the Cretaceous Limestone of the Paluxy River Bed, Texas', *Journal of Geological Education*, vol. 31 (1983), pp.111-123.
17. Walter E. Lammerts (ed.), *Why Not Creation?* (Presbyterian & Reformed, 1970), pp.186-193.
18. Reported by Alan Hayward in *Creation and Evolution*, (Triangle, SPCK, London, 1985), pp.150-151.
19. Mary D. Leakey, 'Footprints in the Ashes of Time' *National Geographic Magazine*, vol. 155 (April 1979), pp.446-457.
20. Leakey, 'Footprints in the Ashes of Time'.
21. 'First Glimpse of a Stone-Age Tribe', *National Geographic*, vol. 140 (December 1971), pp. 881-882.
22. The programme was called *Scandal of the Lost Tribe* and it was first broadcast on 23 August 1988 by ITV.

Chapter 5

1. *Darwin Up To Date* (A New Scientist Guide), ed. Jeremy Cherfas, (IPC Magazines, London, 1982), pp.5-7.
2. David Attenborough, *Life on Earth* (Collins/BBC,1979), p.14.
3. Michael Ruse, 'Creation Science: the Ultimate Fraud' in *Darwin Up To Date*, pp.7-11.
4. Diane Eager, 'C345 Keeps You Alive!' *Creation Ex Nihilo*, vol. 8, no.4, (September 1986), pp.12-14.
5. Malcolm Bowden, *Ape-Men - Fact or Fallacy?*, pp.142-144. Francis Hitching, *Neck of the Giraffe*, pp. 200-205.
6. Quoted in J. Assmuth, *Haeckel's Frauds and Forgeries* (London, 1918), p.63.
7. See for example, G. Rager, 'Human Embryology and the Law of Biogenesis', *Rivista di Biologia - Biology Forum* vol. 79 (no.4) (1986), pp.449-465.
8. *Archiv für anthropologie, dritter band*, Braunschweig, pp.301-302.
9. Hitching, *Neck of the Giraffe*, p.204.
10. Assmuth, *Haeckel's Frauds and Forgeries*, p.10.
11. Bowden, *Ape-man, Fact or Fallacy*, p.142.
12. Assmuth, *Haeckel's Frauds and Forgeries*, pp.14-15.
13. Rager, 'Human Embroyology and the law of Biogenesis'.
14. Published in 1895, pp.200-202.
15. S. R. Scadding, 'Do Vestigial Organs Provide Evidence For Evolution?' *Evolutionary Theory*, vol. 5 (May 1981) pp.173-176.
16. J. N. Moore & H. S. Slusher (eds.) *Biology - A Search For Order In*

Complexity, (Zondervan, Grand Rapids, Michigan, 1974), p.434.
17. Scadding, 'Do Vestigial Organs provide Evidence for Evolution?'
18. Taken from *Biology, A Search for Order in Complexity,* p.432.
19. Hitching, *Neck of the Giraffe,* pp.62-63.
20. S. L. Miller, *Science,* vol. 117 (1953), pp.528-529.
21. Leslie Orgel, 'Darwinism at the Very Beginning of Life', *Darwin Up To Date,* pp.15-17.
22. Fred Hoyle and Chandra Wickramasinghe, *Evolution From Space* (Dent, London, 1981).
23. Harold F. Blum, *American Scientist,* vol. 43, (1955), p.595.
24. Hitching, *Neck of the Giraffe,* p.66
25. Sidney W. Fox (ed.) *The Origins of Prebiological Systems and Their Molecular Matrices* (Academic Press, New York, 1965), p.359.
26. R. E. Dickerson, 'Chemical Evolution and the Origin of Life', *Scientific American,* vol. 239, no.3 (September 1978), p.62.
27. Orgel, 'Darwinism at the Very Beginning of Life'.
28. D. T. Gish, *Speculations and Experiments Related to Theories on the Origin of Life: A Critique* (Institute For Creation Research, San Diego, 1972).
29. Hitching, *Neck of the Giraffe* , p.75.
30. John Gribbin, *Genesis* (Oxford University Press, 1982), pp.191-192.
31. A. E. Wilder-Smith, *He Who Thinks Has To Believe* (Master Books, San Diego, 1981).
32. R. L. Cann, M. Stoneking and A. C. Wilson, 'Mitochondrial DNA and Human Evolution', *Nature,* vol. 325 (1987), pp.31-37.
33. Nancy Darrall, 'Maybe Eve Really Did Exist!' *Origins,* vol. 2, no.4 (April 1988), pp.5-7.
34. Darrall, 'Maybe Eve Really Did Exist!'
35. F. J. Ayala, 'The Mechanisms of Evolution', *Scientific American,* vol. 239 (September 1978), pp.56-69.
36. Acts 17: 26.
37. Colin Patterson, *Evolution* (British Museum [Natural History], London, 1978), p.139.
38. Gary E. Parker, 'Creation, Mutation and Variation', *ICR Impact* No.89 (November 1980).
39. Ayala, 'Mechanisms of Evolution'.
40. Parker, 'Creation, Mutation and Variation'.
41. Parker, 'Creation, Mutation and Variation'.
42. Parker, 'Creation, Mutation and Variation'.

Chapter 6
1. For a detailed analysis of the length and meaning of these days, see pp. 31-37 of my book *How Old is the Earth?* (Evangelical Press, 1985). Suffice it to say here that these days are literal.
2. E. J. Young, *Studies in Genesis One,* in the International Library of Philosophy and Theology: Biblical & Theological Studies, edited by J. Marcellus Kik (Presbyterian and Reformed, 1973), p.105.
3. J. P. Versteeg, *Is Adam a 'Teaching Model' in the New Testament?* (Presbyterian and Reformed, 1978), p.31.
4. Other ancient creation myth accounts are given in Appendix III of P. J. Wiseman, *Clues to Creation in Genesis* (Marshall, Morgan & Scott, 1977), pp.223-228.

5. P. J. Wiseman gives a detailed comparison of the Babylonian creation myth *(Enuma elish)* and the Genesis account of creation on pp.156-160.
6. Quoted in *Tyndale New Testament Commentaries: Romans* by Professor F. F. Bruce (Tyndale Press, 1963), p.127.
7. The alternative rendering of verse 7 has been quoted.
8. J. G. Vos quoted in *The Bible League Quarterly* (Oct. - Dec. 1974), p.284.
9. Contrary to cartoons, jokes and music hall songs, Eve was not tempted to eat an apple. It was not the fruit of an apple tree, but the fruit of the tree of the knowledge of good and evil. You may wonder why then this fruit is so often thought of as being an apple. The answer is because the Latin for evil is *malus* and the Latin word for apple is also *malus*. Because the word *malus* appeared in the Latin Vulgate Bible in the phrase 'tree of knowledge of good and evil', people began to think of an apple tree when they read this phrase.
10. A. J. Monty White, *How Old is the Earth?* (Evangelical Press, 1985), pp.21-30.
11. This summary has been taken from Alan Hayward, *Creation and Evolution: the Facts and Fallacies* (Triangle, SPCK, 1985), p.193. Alan Hayward is not a theistic evolutionist.
12. R. J. Berry, 'I Believe in God...Maker of Heaven and Earth' in *Creation and Evolution* ed. by Derek Burke (IVP, 1985), p.99.
13. Berry, 'I Believe in God...'
14. Berry, 'I Believe in God...'
15. Personal communication.
16. E. K. Victor Pearce, *Who Was Adam?* (Paternoster Press, 1969).
17. Weston W. Fields, *Unformed and Unfilled* (Presbyterian and Reformed, 1976).
18. For example, Alan Hayward, *Creation and Evolution: the Facts and Fallacies*, pp.181-183. Alan Hayward does not, however, believe in the gap theory.

Chapter 7
1. Genesis 2: 16-20; 3: 8-19.
2. Lewis Thomas, *The Lives of a Cell* (Futura, London, 1976), p.105.
3. Richard E. Leakey & Roger Lewin, *Origins* p.184.
4. 'Are Those Apes Really Talking?' *Time* (10 March 1980), pp.50-51.
5. Thomas M. Brown Jr, 'Race and Interracial Marriage: A Biblical Survey and Perspective', *Creation Social Science and Humanities Quarterly*, vol. 7(1) (Fall 1984), pp.5-14.
6. Brown, 'Race and Interracial Marriage'.
7. Henry M. Morris, *The Genesis Record* (Evangelical Press, 1977), pp.143-144.
8. Wiseman, *Clues to Creation in Genesis* .
9. Told in 'The Tragic Journey of Burke and Wills', *National Geographic* , vol. 155 (February 1979), p.184.
10. Chalcedon Report Number 165 (May 1979). Obtainable from Chalcedon, P.O. Box 158, Vallecito, California 95251, U.S.A.
11. Published by Chalcedon.
12. William Hendriksen, *New Testament Commentary: The Gospel of Luke* (The Banner of Truth Trust, Edinburgh, 1979), p.237.
13. Eryl Davies, *Condemned for Ever!* (Evangelical Press, 1987).